# MRS. C. H. S~~~~~

BY

## CHARLES RAY,

*Author of " The Life of Charles Haddon Spurgeon."*

# Pilgrim PUBLICATIONS,
## Pasadena, Texas 77501

Original Passmore & Alabaster Edition, 1903.
Pilgrim editions: 1973, 1979, 2003.
ISBN 1-56186-305-X

Very sincerely yours

S. Spurgeon

# PREFACE

IT has been felt that a short biography of Mrs. C. H. Spurgeon would be appreciated by the many thousands who have received help through her Book Fund and its auxiliary branches, and by the still greater number of persons who have been incited to increased efforts in the service of Christ through her inspiring example. Mrs. Spurgeon was indeed a wonderful woman, and if this little book arouses interest in the Book Fund where hitherto its unique work was unknown, and encourages invalid Christians and others to take up some work for their Master by showing them the tremendous possibilities that lie in the power of the weakest, it will have achieved its purpose.

CHARLES RAY.

*Forest Gate,*

*Essex.*

*November,* 1903.

# CONTENTS.

Mrs. C. H. Spurgeon.

Born January 15, 1832. Died October 22, 1903.

*In a few days it will be out of my power to present anything to Miss Thompson. Let this be a remembrance of our happy meetings & sweet conversations*

*Dec 22 /55 .*

*C. H. Spurgeon*

Inscription on the fly-leaf of a copy of *The Pulpit Library*,
the first published volume of C. H. Spurgeon's Sermons,
presented to Mrs. Spurgeon just before marriage.

FACSIMILES OF LOVERS' KEEPSAKES.

THE FAMILY REGISTER.

Charles Haddon Spurgeon and Susannah Thompson were by the gracious arrangement of Divine Providence, most happily married at New Park Street Chapel by Dr Alexander Fletcher on Tuesday, January 8th 1856.

"And as year rolls after year
"Each to other still more dear

EXCEPT THE LORD BUILD THE HOUSE.

THEY LABOR IN VAIN THAT BUILD

VAN DARGENT

C. H. Spurgeon and his wife in their garden
soon after marriage.

OUR FIRST HOME (NO. 217, NEW KENT ROAD, LONDON).

HUSBAND AND WIFE AT HOME.

FATHER AND SONS IN THE GARDEN.

THE YOUNG LECTURERS AND THEIR DEAR MOTHER.

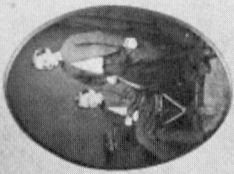

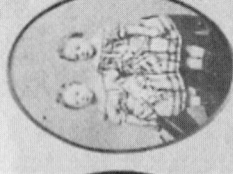

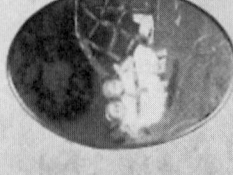

THE SPURGEON SONS : TWENTY-ONE YEARLY PICTURES.

# The New "Helensburgh House," Nightingale Lane.

THE NEW "HELENSBURGH HOUSE" (FRONT VIEW).

C. H. SPURGEON ON THE BALCONY OF THE NEW "HELENSBURGH HOUSE."

WESTWOOD HOUSE, RESIDENCE OF MR. SPURGEON.

SILVER WEDDING PORTRAITS.

Mrs. C. H. Spurgeon in her boudoir, from a photograph taken
at the time of her husband's jubilee.

MRS. SPURGEON'S BOOK FUND ROOM ON "PACKING-DAY.

(*Supplement to "The Sword and the Trowel," May,* 1897.)

**Mrs. Spurgeon shovels first ground for erecting Beulah Chapel, memorial to CHS.**

# INTRODUCTION

THE position of the wife of a great man and particularly of a great minister, is not only one of rare difficulty but calls for an exercise of unselfishness and self-effacement which is quite contrary to the natural instincts of human nature. The lady who would be a true helpmeet to the popular preacher and God-ordained pastor must to a very large extent sink her own individuality and claims and become absorbed in those of her husband. She must be prepared to part often with the one she loves best on earth, in order that he may go to fulfil his solemn engagements untrammelled by domestic repinings; she must render every assistance in her power and yet not expect to reap the praise from men, which is rightly her due; she must initiate and carry through new plans of Christian effort and be satisfied that they shall be regarded as nothing more than a legitimate part of her husband's ministry; and she must take upon her shoulders a load of responsibility, which the ordinary wife knows nothing of and which amid such a multitude of duties might well overwhelm a strong and vigorous man. If it be true in a general sense that "Whoso findeth a wife findeth a good thing and obtaineth favour of the Lord," how much more must it be the case with the minister who is encouraged and helped by his partner in life. The members of the Christian churches little know what they owe to the wives of their pastors and when, by way of faint praise, they oftentimes declare that the lady of the manse has "done what she could," the expression usually implies a qualification that the work might have been greater or better. How many of those who thus look with a more or less supercilious eye upon the work of the minister's wife do a tithe of the good in the world which can be placed to her credit?

No grander example of the possibilities which the position of a preacher's wife affords, could be offered to her sisters of the manse or to the world at large than Mrs. C. H. Spurgeon, whose death on October 22nd, 1903, has left the Church poorer than it yet realises. Called to a position of rare difficulty at an early age, her husband already raised on dazzling heights of popularity, which few could have endured without being lifted up with pride, it was an ordeal for the retiring girl to be thus suddenly thrust into prominence. Then when the storms of abuse and slander broke on her loved one's head, she might well have been crushed and broken, but she bore up and by her words of comfort, her strong affection and her piety and faith, helped him to weather the gale. In every branch of his work she threw her heart and soul, she stinted herself to render financial assistance to the various causes, and to the smallest detail acted with her husband as a faithful steward of the God in whom she trusted. Never did woman fulfil the marriage vow more faithfully. In sickness and in health, through good report and evil, she was ever his support and it would be difficult to find anywhere another woman, who in spite of adverse circumstances and conditions, ill-health and infirmity, did such monumental work for God and man as Susannah Spurgeon. Her life was one long self-sacrifice. She need not have expended the strength she so much required for herself; no one would have blamed the invalid for seeking comfort in rest, but what she did, she did with a will and as "unto the Lord." Her life is a brilliant example of what can be done by a weak woman who devotes herself to the service of the Master and not only as the wife of Charles Haddon Spurgeon will Mrs. Spurgeon live green in the memory of all true Christians, but as herself, as the woman who found solace in suffering by ministering to the needs of others, she will stand out through all time.

# CHAPTER I.

## EARLY DAYS.

MRS. SPURGEON was born on January 15th, 1832, and her girl-hood days were spent partly in the Southern suburbs and partly in the City of London, which had not then, as now, ceased to be residential. In the political world the times were stirring; there were wars and rumours of wars, but probably little of the turmoil of the nations was known to the young maiden, for English girls were not then allowed to read morning and evening newspapers and encouraged to give their opinions upon the latest events of the day. Her father, Mr. R. B. Thompson, and her mother attended New Park Street Chapel, Southwark, from time to time, and their daughter Susannah used to accompany them, so that with the ministry of the Pastor, James Smith (afterwards of Chel-tenham) she was familiar. "A quaint and rugged preacher, but one well versed in the blessed art of bringing souls to Christ," is how Mrs. Spurgeon describes him. "Often had I seen him administer the ordinance of baptism to the candidates, wondering with a tearful longing whether I should ever be able thus to confess my faith in the Lord

Jesus. I can recall the old-fashioned dapper figure of the senior deacon, of whom I stood very much in awe. He was a lawyer and wore the silk stockings and knee-breeches dear to a former generation. When the time came to give out the hymns he mounted an open desk immediately beneath the pulpit; and from where I sat, I had a side view of him. To the best of my remembrance he was a short, stout man, and his rotund body, perched on his undraped legs and clothed in a long-tailed coat, gave him an unmistakeable resemblance to a gigantic robin; and when he chirped out the verses of the hymn in a piping, twittering voice, I thought the likeness was complete!"

Those early experiences at New Park Street Chapel were among the most vivid memories of Mrs. Spurgeon's life.

"Well, also," she continues, "did I know the curious pulpit without any stairs; it looked like a magnified swallow's nest and was entered from behind through a door in the wall. My childish imagination was always excited by the silent and 'creepy' manner in which the minister made his appearance therein. One moment the big box would be empty—the next, if I had but glanced down at Bible or hymn-book, and raised my eyes again,—there was the preacher, comfortably seated or standing ready to commence the service! I found it very interesting and though I knew there was a matter-of-fact door, through which the good man stepped into his rostrum, this knowledge was not allowed to interfere with, or even explain the fanciful notions I loved to indulge in concerning that mysterious entrance and exit. It was certainly somewhat singular that, in the very pulpit which had exercised such a charm over me, I should have my first glimpse of the one who was to be the love of my heart, and the light of my earthly life."

The young girl's visits to New Park Street Chapel were no doubt more frequent than they would have been, from the fact that old Mr. and Mrs. Olney were very fond of her and often invited her to visit them. Naturally on Sundays, during these visits, she usually accompanied Mr. and Mrs. Olney to the chapel and thus she had more than one association with the place which was to play so large a part in her after history.

Brought up in a godly family and having earnest Christian friends, Susannah Thompson was not indifferent to the importance of religion in the individual life, but it was by means of a sermon from Romans x. 8, "The word is nigh thee, even in thy mouth, and in thy heart," preached at the old

Poultry Chapel, by the Rev. S. B. Bergne, that the girl was first aroused to a sense of her own personal need of a Saviour. "From that service," she says, "I date the dawning of the true light in my soul. The Lord said to me, through His servant, 'Give Me thy heart,' and, constrained by His love, that night witnessed my solemn resolution of entire surrender to Himself."

In those days there were no Christian Endeavour Societies, and few attempts at encouraging young converts to engage in service for their Lord. The lack of communion with kindred youthful spirits and the absence of Christian work to occupy the mind and lead to further knowledge of God, were, no doubt, more or less responsible for a state of coldness and indifference which in a short time took the place of the joy and gladness of soul that had followed conversion. "Seasons of darkness, despondency and doubt, had passed over me," she says, "but I had kept all my religious experiences carefully concealed in my own breast," the hesitancy and reserve in this respect being the cause, in Mrs. Spurgeon's judgment, of the sickly and sleepy condition of her soul. It was at this juncture that she first came under the influence of the man who was in a few years to become more dear to her than all others.

## CHAPTER II.

### FIRST CONTACT WITH C. H. SPURGEON.

ON the morning of Sunday, December 18th, 1853, Charles Haddon Spurgeon, then a *gauche* country youth of nineteen years, preached for the first time in the pulpit of New Park Street Chapel. Susannah Thompson was staying with old Mr. and Mrs. Olney, but she did not go to the service although like many others the much-talked of experiment of asking a lad from a rural village to occupy the historic pulpit of Benjamin Keach, Dr. Gill and Dr. Rippon interested her. The members of the Olney family when they returned from the morning service, were full of praise for the preacher, and, in common with others of the congregation, they were determined that in the evening the many empty seats which had obviously discouraged and disconcerted the young minister, should be filled. Friends and acquaintances were called upon and urged to go to New Park Street Chapel, with the result that in the evening the church was full.

Susannah Thompson was there, more to please her friends than herself, for having rigid ideas as to the proprieties of the pulpit, she entertained no prepossessions in favour of one—and he a mere youth—who dared to break those proprieties. The chapel was filled, a hush fell upon the multitude, and all eyes, including those of the young maiden, were turned towards the pulpit. At last the door in the wall opened and the preacher entered briskly. Miss Thompson was shocked. This was quite contrary to her ideas of what a preacher should be. Young Charles Haddon Spurgeon was evidently from the country; she could have told that in a moment even if she had not known. His clothes had the village tailor marked upon every part of them; round his neck he wore a great stock of black satin, and in his hand he carried a blue handkerchief with white spots! What business had such a youth in the pulpit of Dr. Gill and Dr. Rippon? and with that thought in her prejudiced mind Susannah Thompson settled down to hear what he had to say.

"Ah!" wrote Mrs. Spurgeon in after years, "how little I then thought that my eyes looked on him who was to be my life's beloved; how little I dreamed of the honour God was preparing for me in the near future! It is a mercy that our lives are not left for us to plan, but that our Father chooses for us; else might we sometimes turn away from our best blessings,

and put from us the choicest and loveliest
gifts of His providence.  For, if the whole
truth be told, I was not at all fascinated
by the young orator's eloquence, while his
countrified manner and speech excited
more regret than reverence.  Alas, for
my vain and foolish heart!  I was not
spiritually-minded enough to understand
his earnest presentation of the Gospel and
his powerful pleading with sinners;—but
the huge black satin stock, the long badly-
trimmed hair, and the blue pocket handkerchief with white spots which he himself
has   so   graphically   described,—these
attracted most of my attention and I fear
awakened some feelings of amusement.
There was only one sentence of the whole
sermon which I carried away with me, and
that solely on account of its quaintness, for
it seemed to me an extraordinary thing for
the preacher to speak of the 'living stones
in the Heavenly Temple perfectly joined
together with the vermilion cement of
Christ's blood.'"

When C. H. Spurgeon finally accepted
the pastorate of New Park Street Chapel,
Miss Thompson often met him at the
house of Mr. and Mrs. Olney, although
neither the preacher nor his wife could ever
recall their first introduction to one another.
The young maiden seems to have soon got
over her prejudices and often went to hear

the new minister. It was not long before his earnest pleadings aroused her and she realised that her life of indifference and non-service was far from being what it should be.

"Gradually I became alarmed at my back-sliding state and then, by a great effort, I sought spiritual help and guidance from Mr. William Olney ('Father' Olney's second son, and my cousin by marriage), who was an active worker in the Sunday School at New Park Street, and a true Mr. Greatheart and comforter of young pilgrims. He may have told the new Pastor about me,—I cannot say;—but one day I was greatly surprised to receive from Mr. Spurgeon an illustrated copy of *The Pilgrim's Progress*, in which he had written the inscription 'Miss Thompson, with desires for her progress in the blessed pilgrimage, from C. H. Spurgeon, April 20th 1854.'

"I do not think," continues Mrs. Spurgeon, "that my beloved had at that time any other thought concerning me than to help a struggling soul Heavenward; but I was greatly impressed by his concern for me, and the book became very precious as well as helpful. By degrees, though with much trembling, I told him of my state before God; and he gently led me, by his preaching, and by his conversations,

through the power of the Holy Spirit to
the cross of Christ for the peace and pardon
my weary soul was longing for."

From this time the intimacy and friendship of the young couple grew, although
on Miss Thompson's part, at any rate, there
was no thought of love. She tells us, however, that she was happier than she had
been since the days at the Poultry Chapel
when she was first brought to the feet of
Christ, and it is clear that the preacher who
had taken London by storm, had proved of
real spiritual blessing to this quiet young
girl who now sat pretty regularly in his
congregation.

Miss Thompson
with desires for her progress
in the blessed pilgrimage.
from
C H Spurgeon
Ap 20. 1854.

Inscription in a copy of "Pilgrim's Progress," given by
C. H. Spurgeon to the lady who afterwards became his
wife, with a view to helping her spiritually.

# CHAPTER III.

## THE DAWNING OF LOVE.

THE manner and circumstances in which C. H. Spurgeon declared his love to Miss Thompson were very characteristic of the man. At the opening of the Crystal Palace, at Sydenham, on June 10th, 1854, a large party of friends connected with the New Park Street Chapel was present, including the preacher and the young girl to whom he had rendered such valuable spiritual help.

"We occupied some raised seats," says Mrs. Spurgeon, "at the end of the Palace where the great clock is now fixed. As we sat there talking, laughing and amusing ourselves as best we could, while waiting for the procession to pass by, Mr. Spurgeon handed me a book into which he had been occasionally dipping, and, pointing to some particular lines said, 'What do you think of the poet's suggestion in those verses?' The volume was Martin Tupper's *Proverbial Philosophy*, then recently published, and already beginning to feel the stir of the breezes of adverse criticism, which afterwards gathered into a howling tempest of disparagement and scathing sarcasm.

No thought had I for authors and their
woes at that moment. The pointing finger
guided my eyes to the chapter ' On
Marriage,' of which the opening sentences
ran thus : —

"'Seek a good wife of thy God, for she is the
    best gift of His providence ;
Yet ask not in bold confidence that which
    He hath not promised :
Thou knowest not His good will ; be thy
    prayer then submissive thereunto ;
And leave thy petition to His mercy
    assured that He will deal well with thee.
If thou art to have a wife of thy youth, she
    is now living on the earth ;
Therefore think of her and pray for her
    weal ! '

"' Do you pray for him who is to be
your husband ? ' said a soft, low voice in my
ear,—so soft that no one else heard the
whisper.

"I do not remember that the question
received any vocal answer ; but my fast-
beating heart, which sent a tell-tale flush to
my cheeks, and my downcast eyes, which
feared to reveal the light which at once
dawned in them, may have spoken a
language which love understood. From
that moment a very quiet and subdued
little maiden sat by the young Pastor's side,
and while the brilliant procession passed
round the Palace, I do not think she took

so much note of the glittering pageant
defiling before her, as of the crowd of
newly-awakened emotions which were
palpitating within her heart. Neither the
book nor its theories were again alluded to,
but when the formalities of the opening
were over, and the visitors were allowed to
leave their seats, the same low voice
whispered again, ' Will you come and walk
round the Palace with me?' How we
obtained leave of absence from the rest of
the party, I know not; but we wandered
together for a long time, not only in the
wonderful building itself, but in the gardens
and even down to the lake, beside which
the colossal forms of extinct monsters were
being cunningly modelled." "During that
walk on that memorable day in June, I
believe," wrote Mrs. Spurgeon, a few years
before her death, "God Himself united our
hearts in indissoluble bonds of true
affection, and, though we knew it not, gave
us to each other for ever. From that time
our friendship grew apace and quickly
ripened into deepest love,—a love which
lives in my heart to-day as truly, aye, and
more solemnly and strongly than it did in
those early days; for, though God has
seen fit to call my beloved up to higher
service, He has left me the consolation of
still loving him with all my heart, and
believing our love shall be perfected when

we meet in that blessed land where Love reigns supreme and eternal."

Would anyone but Charles Haddon Spurgeon have whispered his love in the midst of a crowd, and have made it known by asking the lady of his choice to pray for her future husband?

# CHAPTER IV.

## COURTSHIP DAYS.

LESS than two months after the incident at the Crystal Palace, C. H. Spurgeon formally proposed for the hand of Susannah Thompson. They were in the little old-fashioned garden of the girl's grandfather, with its high brick walls, straight, formal gravel paths and small lawn,—"rather a dreary and unromantic place for a declaration of love," as Mrs. Spurgeon described it. "But," she says, "people are not particularly careful as to the selection of their surroundings at such a moment, and do not often take pains to secure a delightful background to the picture, which will for ever be photographed on their hearts. To this day I think of that old garden as a sacred place, a paradise of happiness, since there my beloved sought me for his very own, and told me how much he loved me. Though I thought I knew this already, it was a very different matter to hear him say it, and I trembled and was silent for very joy and gladness." What words the lover used we are not told, but Mrs. Spurgeon has declared that the verbal confession was

"wonderful," and writing forty years afterwards she could ask, "Was there ever quite
such bliss on earth before?" They were
one in heart, in soul, in inclination, and even
at this stage the great preacher had com-
municated to his fiancée much of his own
spirituality and earnestness. There was
more than mere earthly affection in their
love for one another, and both felt that
indeed the finger of God had marked out
a united course for them. "To me," says
Mrs. Spurgeon, "it was a time as *solemn*
as it was sweet; and with a great awe in
my heart, I left my beloved and, hastening
to the house and to an upper room, I knelt
before God and praised and thanked Him
with happy tears for His great mercy in
giving me the love of so good a man. If
I had known then *how* good he was and
how great he would become, I should have
been overwhelmed, not so much with the
happiness of being his, as with the responsibility which such a position would entail."
In the diary which the young girl kept she
thus made a record of that memorable day
—August 2nd, 1854,—"It is impossible to
write down all that occurred this morning.
I can only adore in silence the mercy of my
God, and praise Him for all His benefits."

Miss Thompson now attended New Park
Street Chapel pretty regularly, and before
long she sought for membership and

became a candidate for baptism. The preacher asked her to write out her confession of faith, probably for his own personal perusal only, and this she did in a manner so satisfactory as to elicit a letter from him in which his joy at the work of grace in her soul can scarcely find utterance. "Oh! I could weep for joy (as I certainly am doing now)," he wrote, "to think that my beloved can so well testify to a work of grace in her soul. I knew you were *really* a child of God, but I did not think you had been led in such a path. I see my Master has been ploughing deep and it is the deep-sown seed, struggling with the clods, which now makes your bosom heave with distress. If I know anything of spiritual symptoms, I think I know a cure for you. Your position is not the sphere for earnest labour for Christ. You have done all you could in more ways than one; but you are not brought into actual contact either with the saints or with the sinful, sick or miserable, whom you could serve. Active service brings with it warmth and this tends to remove doubting, for our works thus become evidences of our calling and election.

"I flatter no one, but allow me to say, honestly, that few cases which have come under my notice are so satisfactory as yours. Mark, I write not now as your

The volumes making up a complete set of Calvin were a gift to me from my own most dear, & tender wife. Blessed may she be among women. How much of comfort & strength she has ministered unto me it is not in my power to estimate. She has been to me God's best earthly gift, & not a little even of heavenly treasure has come to me by her means. She has often been as an angel of God unto me.

C. H. Spurgeon

Inscription on the fly-leaf of the first volume of C. H. Spurgeon's set of Calvin's Commentories.

*admiring friend*, but impartially as your Pastor.    If the Lord had intended your destruction, He would not have told you such things as these, nor would He enable you so unreservedly to cast yourself upon His faithful promise.  As I hope to stand at the bar of God, clear of the blood of all men, it would ill become me to flatter ; and as I love you with the deepest and purest affection, far be it from me to trifle with your immortal interests ; but I will say again that my gratitude to God ought to be great, as well on my own behalf as yours, that you have been so deeply schooled in the lessons of the heart and have so frequently looked into the charnel-house of your own corruption.    There are other lessons to come, that you may be thoroughly furnished ; but, oh! my dear one, how good to learn the first lesson well!  I loved you once, but feared you might not be an heir of Heaven ;—God in His mercy showed me that you were indeed *elect*.   I then thought I might without sin reveal my affection to you,—but up to the time I saw your note, I could not imagine that you had seen such great sights and were so thoroughly versed in soul-knowledge.  God is good, very good, infinitely good.  Oh, how I prize this last gift, because I now know, more than ever, that the Giver loves the gift, and so I may

love it too, but only in subservience to Him.
Dear purchase of a Saviour's blood, you
are to me a Saviour's gift, and my heart is
full to overflowing with the thought of such
continued goodness. I do not wonder at
His goodness, for it is just like Him; but I
cannot but lift up my voice of joy at His
manifold mercies.

"Whatever befall us, trouble and adver-
sity, sickness or death, we need not fear
a final separation, either from each other
or our God. I am glad you are not here
just at this moment, for I feel so deeply that
I could only throw my arms around you
and weep. May the choicest favours be
thine, may the Angel of the Covenant be
thy companion, may thy supplications be
answered, and may thy conversation be
with Jesus in Heaven! Farewell; unto
my God and my father's God I commend
you. Yours, with pure and holy affection
as well as terrestrial love, C. H. Spurgeon."

Surely a remarkable lover's letter and
one which speaks volumes as to the
character of both the writer and the
recipient. C. H. Spurgeon had said that
there were other lessons to come that she
might be thoroughly furnished, and this
was true not only in her soul's experience,
but also in the preparation and schooling
for the position of a minister's wife. Some
of these lessons, Mrs. Spurgeon herself has

told us, were far from pleasing, but she learned them well, and became the stronger and more earnest for the teaching. At times the preacher would be so absorbed in his great mission, when about to preach, that on his fiancée entering the vestry, he would fail to recognise her and merely greet her with a handshake as if she were some casual acquaintance or visitor. Once there was a more trying experience still. C. H. Spurgeon was to preach in a large hall at Kennington on a certain afternoon and Miss Thompson accompanied him thither in a cab. The pavement outside the building was thronged with people as were also the entrance hall and staircase leading to the auditorium, and the maiden had hard work in struggling through the mass of people and trying to keep near her lover. Suddenly he turned in at a side door on the landing, leaving Miss Thompson to manage as best she could in the throng eagerly pressing forward to get into the hall. The burden of souls was resting heavily upon the preacher, and occupied with the momentousness of the message he was to deliver, he had forgotten all about his poor fiancée.

Miss Thompson's feelings at what she considered an unpardonable slight, may easily be imagined. "At first," she says, "I was utterly bewildered, and then, I am

sorry to have to confess, I was *angry*." She
at once returned home, without making any
further effort to get to a seat, her indignation and grief increasing momentarily.
But the young girl possessed that best
of gifts a wise and loving mother, who with
the greatest tact sought to soothe her
daughter's ruffled spirits. "She wisely
reasoned," says Mrs. Spurgeon, "that my
chosen husband was no ordinary man, that
his whole life was absolutely dedicated to
God and His service, and that I must never,
*never* hinder him by trying to put myself
first in his heart. Presently, after much
good and loving counsel, my heart grew
soft, and I saw I had been very foolish and
wilful; and then a cab drew up at the door
and dear Mr. Spurgeon came running into
the house in great excitement, calling,
' Where's Susie? I have been searching
for her everywhere and cannot find her;
has she come back by herself?' My dear
mother went to him, took him aside and
told him all the truth; and, I think, when
he realized the state of things, she had to
soothe him also; for he was so innocent
at heart of having offended me in any way,
that he must have felt I had done him an
injustice in thus doubting him. At last,
mother came to fetch me to him, and I
went downstairs. Quietly he let me tell
him how indignant I had felt, and then he

repeated mother's little lesson, assuring me of his deep affection for me, but pointing out that, before all things, he was *God's servant*, and I must be prepared to yield my claims to His. I never forgot the teaching of that day; I had learned my hard lesson *by heart*, for I do not recollect ever again seeking to assert my right to his time and attention when any service for God demanded them."

The incident closed happily with a cosy tea at her mother's house, and Mrs. Spurgeon speaks of the sweet calm which reigned in the hearts of all after the storm of the afternoon. When a few weeks later the preacher was to fulfil an engagement at Windsor he wrote and asked his fiancée to accompany him, adding, "Possibly, I may be again inattentive to you if you do go; but this will be nice for us both,— that 'Charles' may have space for mending, and that 'Susie' may exhibit her growth in knowledge of his character, by patiently enduring his failings."

In April, 1855, Miss Thompson paid a week's visit to Colchester in company with her fiancé, to be introduced to his parents and family. It was a very happy holiday, the fact that the lovers were together all day, and that the Rev. John Spurgeon and his wife "welcomed and petted" their future daughter-in-law, being the principal contributory causes. When the young minister was in London he had little time for courtship, and when he did visit his fiancée at her Brixton home he usually took proofs of a sermon with him to revise for the press. "I learned to be quiet and to mind my own business while this important work was going on," says Mrs. Spurgeon. "It was good discipline for the Pastor's intended wife."

Even in these early days C. H. Spurgeon was abused in the press, and he found some consolation in writing to his fiancée, who did much to comfort and sustain him. "I am down in the valley," he says, in a letter of May, 1855; "partly because of two desperate attacks in *The Sheffield Independent* and *The Empire*, and partly because I cannot find a subject. Yet faith fails not. I know and believe the promise and am not afraid to rest upon it. All the scars I receive are scars of honour; so faint heart, on to the battle! My love, were you here, how you would comfort me; but since you are not I shall do what is better still, go upstairs alone and pour out my grief into my Saviour's ear."

About this time Miss Thompson's parents removed from Brixton to Falcon Square in the City of London, and the lovers saw more of one another, than they had hitherto done. The young maiden

commenced to help her future husband in
his literary work and very proud she was
of the honour and trust thus implied,
although the responsibility seemed at first
overwhelming.  His wonderful popularity
and success as a preacher naturally delighted
and awed the timid maiden, but with the
pleasure was mingled something of anxiety
and distress, for the strain on the preacher's
physical power when addressing the large
congregations that gathered at Exeter Hall
was tremendous, and his fiancée, sitting
watching him from the body of the Hall,
often felt she must rush to his succour.
"A glass of Chili vinegar," she says,
"always stood on a shelf under the desk
before him, and I knew what to expect
when he had recourse to that remedy.  Oh,
how my heart ached for him!  What self-
control I had to exercise to appear calm
and collected and keep quietly in my seat
up in that little side gallery!  How I
longed to have the *right* to go and comfort
and cheer him when the service was over!
But I had to walk away, as other people
did,—I who belonged to him and was
closer to his heart than anyone there!  It
was severe discipline for a young and
loving spirit."

When the preacher went to Scotland in
July, 1855, his first long journey by rail, he
wrote many letters to his fiancée, giving

her an account of the services he conducted,
and the crowds who flocked to hear him,
and asking her to pray that he might be
sustained and helped, and his preaching
blessed to the souls of the people. "I
shall feel deeply indebted to you," he says
in one note, "if you will pray very
earnestly for me. I fear I am not so full
of love to God as I used to be. I lament
my sad decline in spiritual things. You
and others have not observed it but I am
now conscious of it, and a sense thereof has
put bitterness in my cup of joy. Oh!
what is it to be popular, to be successful,
to have abundance, even to have love so
sweet as yours,—if I should be left of God
to fall and to depart from His ways? I
tremble at the giddy height on which I
stand, and could wish myself unknown, for
indeed, I am unworthy of all my honours
and my fame. I trust I shall now commence anew and wear no longer the linsey-
woolsey garment; but, I beseech you,
blend your hearty prayers with mine, that
two of us may be agreed, and thus will you
promote the usefulness and holiness and
happiness of one whom you love."

His affection for the maiden of his
choice grew deeper, if that were possible,
during this absence. "I have had day-
dreams of you while driving along," he
writes in one letter. " I thought you were

very near me.   It is not long, dearest, before I shall again enjoy your sweet society, if the providence of God permits.   I knew I loved you very much before, but now I feel how necessary you are to me ;  and you will not lose much by my absence, if you find me, on my return, more attentive, to your feelings, as well as equally affectionate.    I can now thoroughly sympathize with your tears, because I feel in no little degree that pang of absence which my constant engagements prevented me from noticing when in London.    How then must you, with so much leisure, have felt my absence from you even though you well knew that it was unavoidable on my part!    My darling, accept love of the deepest and purest kind from one who is not prone to exaggerate, but who feels that here there is no room for hyperbole."

It must have been no ordinary woman who could draw such letters from Charles Haddon Spurgeon.

# CHAPTER V.

## MARRIED LIFE.

THE wedding of Susannah Thompson and Charles Haddon Spurgeon took place at New Park Street Chapel, on January 8th, 1856, Dr. Alexander Fletcher, of Finsbury Chapel, officiating. As may be imagined in the case of a man whose name was in everybody's mouth, and whose remarkable work was the topic of discussion up and down the country, it was quite impossible for the wedding to be a quiet one. At a very early hour in the morning people began to gather outside the Chapel, ladies being among the first arrivals, and soon after eight o'clock the crowd had swelled to such proportions, that New Park Street and some adjoining thoroughfares were blocked with people, and traffic was practically at a standstill. A special body of police had to be summoned to prevent accidents. When the chapel doors were at last opened, there was a rush for seats, and in less than half-an-hour the building was filled to its utmost extent. Large numbers who had tickets of admission but arrived late were unable to gain entrance. Many went

home when they found that there was no
chance of their being able to get inside the
chapel, but some thousands still remained
in the streets to see the bride and bridegroom enter and leave.

It must have been a trying ordeal for the
modest and retiring girl.    She had risen
early and spent much time in her bedroom
in private prayer.    Although awed with a
sense of the responsibilities which she was
about to assume, she was "happy beyond
expression" that the Lord had so favoured
her, and on her knees, with no one else near,
she earnestly sought strength and blessing
and guidance   in   the   new life opening
before her.

The dressing for the ceremony did not
take an unconscionable time, as it does with
some maidens, for Susannah Thompson was
very   simply   attired,   and   as   she   drove
through the city to the chapel with her
father the young girl's chief thought was,
"as the passers-by cast astonished glances
at the wedding equipage whether they all
knew what a wonderful bridegroom she
was going to meet."   The crowds standing
in the streets adjoining New Park Street,
bewildered the bride, and she remembered
little more until she was inside the building,
"a large wedding party in the table-pew,
dear old Dr. Alexander Fletcher beaming
benignly   on   the   bride   and   bridegroom

before him, and the deacons endeavouring to calm and satisfy the excited and eager onlookers."

The service was commenced by the congregation singing the hymn, "Salvation, O, the joyful sound!" after which Dr. Fletcher read the hundredth Psalm and prayed for the Divine blessing upon the young couple. The venerable minister then gave a short address and the wedding ceremony was performed in the usual manner. The reading of another lesson, a hymn sung by the congregation and a closing prayer, completed the proceedings, and Mr. and Mrs. Spurgeon, after receiving the congratulations of their friends in the chapel, drove away amid the loud and continued cheering of the crowds gathered outside the building.

A brief honeymoon of ten days was spent in Paris, and as Mrs. Spurgeon had often been to that city before and was a good French scholar, she acted as cicerone to her husband. Together they visited the various churches and palaces and museums, the lady finding a new interest in all these familiar places on account of "those loving eyes that now looked upon them" with her. Years afterwards during one of C. H. Spurgeon's frequent visits to the French capital he wrote to his wife, "My heart flies to you, as I remember my first visit to

this city under your dear guidance.    I
love you now as then, only multiplied many
times."    The happy couple would have
liked to prolong the holiday, but the
preacher was unable to leave his work, and
so they returned to their first united home
—a modest house in New Kent Road,
London, where as in all their future homes,
the best room became the library. "We
never encumbered ourselves," says Mrs.
Spurgeon, "with what a modern writer
calls ' the draw-back of a drawing-room ' ;
perhaps for the good reason that we were
such homely, busy people that we had no
need of so useless a place ;—but more
especially, I think, because the ' best room '
was always felt to belong by right to the
one who ' laboured much in the Lord.'
Never have I regretted this early decision ;
it is a wise arrangement for a minister's
house, if not for any other."

Housekeeping was commenced on a very
modest scale, for C. H. Spurgeon was
keenly anxious to provide a training for
young preachers who needed a course of
education to fit them for the ministry,
and his wife threw herself into the work
with a zeal not less than his own. She
was a splendid manageress, and by means
of rigid economies quite a substantial
amount was saved towards the support and
education of the first student, the success

of this effort leading to the foundation of the Pastors' College. "I rejoice," says Mrs. Spurgeon, "to remember how I shared my beloved's joy when he founded the Institution, and that together we planned and pinched in order to carry out the purpose of his loving heart; it gave me quite a motherly interest in the College, and 'our own men.' The chief difficulty with regard to money mattters in those days was to 'make both ends meet'; we never had enough left over to 'tie a bow and ends'; but I can see now that this was God's way of preparing us to sympathize with and help poor pastors in the years which were to come."

There were times when the devoted couple abstained from almost necessary things in order to have money to help on the work, and to the young wife it must have been truly a period of anxiety when "means were sorely straitened and the coffers of both College and household were well-nigh empty." But there were joys which more than compensated for any cares of this kind. What times of happiness were spent in the little home on Sunday evenings after the duties of the day were done. On his return from Chapel tired by his labours the preacher would enjoy a light repast and then throw himself into an easy chair by the fireside, while his wife sat on a low cushion at his feet reading to him from the pages of George Herbert or some other Christian poet. Or, if the young minister felt that he had not been as earnest in his preaching as he should have been, the poet would give place to Baxter's *Reformed Pastor*, and as the solemn words were read, husband and wife would sob and weep together, he "from the smitings of a very tender conscience towards God," and she because she "loved him and wanted to share his grief."

The constant absences from home of Charles Haddon Spurgeon in fulfilment of his preaching engagements, were sources of sore trial to the young wife. Often tired of waiting in the sitting-room late at night for his return, she would pace up and down the passage, praying that he might he brought back in safety to his home, and with what a thrill of joy and thankfulness did she open the door and welcome him, when his step was heard outside.

Once and once only she broke down, when her dear one was about to leave in the early morning for a distant mission, and the tears could not be kept back. "Wifey," said her husband, "do you think that when any of the children of Israel brought a lamb to the Lord's altar as an offering to Him they stood and wept over it when they had seen it laid there?" and when she replied in the negative he added, tenderly, "Well, don't you see, you are giving me to God in letting me go to preach the Gospel to poor sinners, and do you think He likes to see you cry over your sacrifice?"

"Could ever a rebuke have been more sweetly and graciously given?" says Mrs. Spurgeon. "It sank deep into my heart, carrying comfort with it; and thenceforward when I parted with him, the tears were scarcely ever allowed to show themselves, or if a stray one or two dared to run over the boundaries he would say, 'What! crying over your lamb, wifey!' and this reminder would quickly dry them up, and bring a smile in their place."

One very remarkable incident happened about this time. On a certain Saturday evening C. H. Spurgeon found himself quite unable to get any light upon the text from which he believed he ought to preach on the following morning. Commentaries were consulted, but in vain, and his wife could not help him. The rest of the story shall be told in Mrs. Spurgeon's own words.

"He sat up very late and was utterly worn out and dispirited, for all his efforts to get at the heart of the text were unavailing. I advised him to retire to rest and soothed him by suggesting that if he would try to sleep then, he would probably in the morning feel quite refreshed and

able to study to better purpose. ' If I go
to sleep now, wifey, will you wake me very
early so that I may have plenty of time to
prepare ? '   With my loving assurance that
I would watch the time for him and call
him soon enough, he was satisfied ;  and,
like a trusting, tired child, he laid his head
upon the pillow and slept soundly and
sweetly at once.

"By-and-by a wonderful thing happened.
During the first dawning hours of the
Sabbath, I heard him talking in his sleep,
and roused myself to listen attentively.
Soon I realised that he was going over the
subject of the verse which had been so
obscure to him, and was giving a clear and
distinct exposition of its meaning with
much force and freshness.   I set myself
with almost trembling joy to understand
and follow all that he was saying, for I
knew that if I could but seize and remember
the salient points of the discourse he would
have no difficulty in developing and en-
larging upon them.   Never preacher had
a more eager and anxious hearer !  What
if I should let the precious words slip ?   I
had no means at hand of ' taking notes,'
so, like Nehemiah, ' I prayed to the God
of Heaven,' and asked that I might receive
and retain the thoughts which He had
given to His servant in his sleep, and which
were so singularly entrusted to my keep-

ing.   As I lay repeating over and over
again the chief points I wished to remember, my happiness was very great in antici-
pation of his surprise and delight on
awaking;   but I had kept vigil so long,
cherishing my joy, that I must have been
overcome with slumber just when the usual
time for rising came, for he awoke with a
frightened start, and  seeing the tell-tale
clock, said, ' Oh, wifey, you said you would
wake me very early, and now see the time!
Oh, why did you let me sleep?   What
shall I do?   What shall I do?'  ' Listen,
beloved,' I answered; and I told him all
I had heard.   ' Why! that's just what I
wanted,' he exclaimed; ' that is the  true
explanation of the whole verse!   And you
say I preached it in my sleep?'   ' It is
wonderful,' he repeated again and again,
and we both praised the Lord for so
remarkable a manifestation of His power
and love."

## CHAPTER VI.

### A Dark Shadow.

ON September 20th, 1856, twin sons were born to Mrs. Spurgeon at her home in the New Kent Road, and the joy of husband and wife knew no bounds. Fortunately the event fell upon a Saturday, and C. H. Spurgeon was able to remain indoors from morning to night. With what pride he gazed upon the babes, and how tenderly he comforted his wife and spoke of the new and happy responsibility which they now had to fulfil! The boys were named Charles and Thomas, and from the first there was a tacit understanding and desire that they should be devoted to the service of God. No cloud that could mar the happiness and joy of the home seemed visible, and there was a holy peace brooding over the little family for which husband and wife repeatedly and devoutly thanked their Lord.

But suddenly and without warning, when things seemed at their brightest, the black shadow of a dreadful sorrow was cast over the young and happy lives, and the faith of the wife and mother must have been such as that which the prophets of old possessed or she would have been distraught. Exactly a month had elapsed since the birth of her boys. She was still very weak although able to leave her room, and on a certain Sunday evening, was lying upon the couch in the little sitting room of her home. That evening, October 19th, 1856, was to become a terrible memory in the lives of husband and wife, but at that time no dread was entertained, at any rate on the part of Mrs. Spurgeon, and there was every prospect that her husband was to have another of those triumphs in the service of His master, which had followed in constant succession since his advent to London.

The young minister was to preach for the first time in the Surrey Gardens Music Hall, where, later in the evening, owing to the machinations of evil-disposed persons, a scene of death and desolation resulted. There had been prayer at home, and with his wife's parting benediction, the young minister set out for the Hall. She lay at home thinking of the great task and praying that the Lord would bless His message to the assembled thousands. Then her mind reverted to her children: "I was dreaming of all sorts of lovely possibilities and pleasures," says Mrs. Spurgeon, "when I heard a carriage stop at the gate. It was far too early for my husband to come

home and I wondered who my unexpected
visitor could be.    Presently one of the
deacons was ushered into the room, and I
saw at once, from his manner, that something unusual had happened.   I besought
him to tell me all quickly and he did so,
kindly, and with much sympathy; and he
kneeled by the couch and prayed that we
might have grace and strength to bear the
terrible trial which had so suddenly come
upon us.   But how thankful I was when
he went away!   I wanted to be alone, that
I might cry to God in this hour of darkness
and death!  When my beloved was brought
home he looked a wreck of his former self,
—an hour's agony of mind had changed
his whole appearance and bearing.   The
night that ensued was one of weeping and
wailing   and   indescribable   sorrow.    He
refused to be comforted.    I thought the
morning would never break; and when it
did come it brought no relief.

"The Lord has mercifully blotted out
from my mind most of the details of the
time of grief which followed when my
beloved's anguish was so deep and violent
that reason seemed to totter in her throne,
and we sometimes feared he would never
preach again.   It was truly 'the valley of
the shadow of death' through which we
then walked; and, like poor Christian, we
here 'sighed bitterly' for the pathway was

so dark 'that ofttimes when we lifted up
our foot to set forward, we knew not where
or upon what we should set it next."

The story of the disaster at the Music
Hall is too well-known to need any des-
cription here, but how many women in Mrs.
Spurgeon's delicate condition could have
borne the terrible trouble as she did, and
not only have fulfilled the duties of a
mother but proved a comfort and stay to
her husband in his mental anguish?

C. H. Spurgeon was taken by friends to
Croydon where he stayed in the house of
Mr. Winsor, one of his deacons, and Mrs.
Spurgeon with the babies joined him there.
It was hoped that the rest and the change
of scene would aid in the restoration of his
mental equilibrium, and although at first
his spirit seemed to be imprisoned in darkness, light at last broke in. "We had been
walking together as usual" (in the garden);
says Mrs. Spurgeon, "he restless and
anguished; I, sorrowful and amazed,
wondering what the end of these things
would be; when at the foot of the steps
which gave access to the house, he stopped
suddenly, and turned to me, and, with the
old sweet light in his eyes (ah! how
grievous had been its absence!), he said,
'Dearest, how foolish I have been! Why!
what does it matter what becomes of me,
if the Lord shall but be glorified?'—and

he repeated with eagerness and intense emphasis, Philippians ii. 9-11 : ' Wherefore God also hath highly exalted Him and given Him a name which is above every name ; that at the Name of Jesus every knee should bow, of things in Heaven, and things in earth and things under the earth, and that every tongue should confess that Jesus Christ is Lord to the glory of God the Father.' ' If Christ be exalted,' he said,—and his face glowed with holy fervour,—' let Him do as He pleases with me ; my one prayer shall be, that I may die to self and live wholly for Him and for His honour ; Oh, wifey, I see it all now ! Praise the Lord with me ! ' "

The husband having recovered his peace of mind, and the wife being strengthened in body, it was decided, while at Croydon, to dedicate the twin sons to the Lord and His service. A number of friends were invited, and the time was spent in prayer and praise, the babies being carried round the room at the conclusion, so that they might be kissed and blessed by those present. Surely those prayers have been answered many times over in the lives of Charles and Thomas Spurgeon.

The Music Hall disaster called forth the virulent abuse of a certain section of the Press, and the preacher collected the newspaper comments and criticisms, as indeed he did throughout his career, and handed them to his wife who stuck them in a book, on the cover of which C. H. Spurgeon himself wrote the title, "Facts, Fiction and Facetiæ." Late in life the devoted wife could smile as she read the unjust and cruel words written by her husband's enemies, "but at the time of their publication what a grievous affliction these slanders were to me," she says. "My heart alternately sorrowed over him and flamed with indignation against his detractors. For a long time I wondered how I could set continual comfort before his eyes, till, at last, I hit upon the expedient of having the following verses printed in large Old English type and enclosed in a pretty Oxford frame : ' Blessed are ye when men shall revile you and persecute you and shall say all manner of evil against you falsely for My sake. Rejoice and be exceeding glad : for great is your reward in Heaven : for so persecuted they the prophets which were before you.'—Matthew v. 11, 12. The text was hung up in our own room and was read over by the dear preacher every morning, —fulfilling its purpose most blessedly, for it strengthened his heart and enabled him to buckle on the invisible armour, whereby he could calmly walk among men, unruffled by their calumnies, and concerned only for their best and highest interests."

# CHAPTER VII.

## HAPPINESS AND SERVICE.

IN 1857 Mr. and Mrs. Spurgeon moved to Helensburgh House, Nightingale Lane, Clapham, a place which they found far more congenial than their first home in the New Kent Road. Clapham was at that time quite a rural district, and, as the house possessed a large garden, the preacher greatly enjoyed the quiet and retirement which he could find there, in the midst of his abundant labours. The country lanes, too, provided delightful walks where the young couple could take recreation without being followed or accosted by admirers, which was not always the case in the neighbourhood of their old residence. Speaking of the garden, Mrs. Spurgeon says : "Oh, what a delightsome place we thought it, though it was a very wilderness through long neglect—the blackberry bushes impertinently asserting themselves to be trees, and the fruit trees running wild for want of the pruning knife. It was all the more interesting to us in this sweet confusion and artlessness because we had the happy task of bringing it gradually into accord with our ideas of what a garden should be. I must admit that we made many absurd mistakes both in house and garden management in those young days of ours; but what did that matter? No two birds ever felt more exquisite joy in building their nest in the fork of a tree-branch than did we in planning and placing, altering and rearranging our pretty country home."

Here, from time to time, a number of distinguished persons visited the minister and his wife, and here, during an illness of the preacher, much pleasant intercourse was had with John Ruskin, who, on one occasion, carried to the house as a present for his friends some charming engravings and some bottles of wine of a rare vintage. Mrs. Spurgeon speaks eloquently of the delightful times spent in her rural Clapham home. "We lived," she says, "in the dear old house in Nightingale Lane for many happy years; and looking back upon them from this distance of time, I think they must have been the least shadowed by care and sorrow of all the years of our married life. We were both young and full of high spirits. We had fairly good health, and devoutly loved each other. Our children grew apace in the sweet country air, and my whole time and strength were given to advance my dear husband's welfare and happiness. I deemed it my joy and privilege to be ever at his side, accompanying him on many of his preaching journeys, nursing him in his occasional illnesses, his delighted companion during his holiday trips, always watching over and tending him with the enthusiasm and sympathy which my great love for him inspired.

"I mention this," she explains, "not to suggest any sort of merit on my part, but simply that I may here record my heartfelt gratitude to God that, for a period of ten blessed years, I was permitted to encircle him with all the comforting care and tender affection which it was in a wife's power to bestow.   Afterwards God ordered it otherwise.   He saw fit to reverse our position to each other ; and for a long season, suffering instead of service became my daily portion, and the care of comforting a sick wife fell upon my beloved."

The garden was a regular rendezvous of songbirds, and during her periods of convalescence it was Mrs. Spurgeon's delight to sit at the window and feed the little creatures.   In this way she made many feathered friends, and the birds would hop around her and feed from her hand, perfect love having quite cast out fear.

Saturday mornings for a good many years were devoted to the students, who used to march down from Mr. Rogers' house, where they resided, to Nightingale

Lane, and there in the garden listen to the addresses of C. H. Spurgeon on theology, preaching and kindred topics, which were really the foundation of the famous " Lectures to Students."

While she enjoyed good health Mrs. Spurgeon took an active part in the work of her husband's church, both at New Park Street Chapel and afterwards at the Metropolitan Tabernacle. She attended the services, often gave spiritual consolation to women and girls who were in trouble about their souls, and assisted the female candidates at the baptismal services. Writing in *The British Banner*, on April 12, 1861, of the first service of this kind in the mammoth building that had just been opened, Dr. Campbell said : —

"The interest of the thing was overpowering. We doubt if it was a whit inferior to that of taking the veil in the Church of Rome. There was the young orator, the idol of the assembly, in the water with a countenance radiant as the light, and there, on the pathway, was Mrs. Spurgeon, a most prepossessing young lady—the admiration of all who beheld her —with courtly dignity and inimitable modesty, kindly leading forward the trembling sisters in succession to her husband, who gently and gracefully took and immersed them with varied remark and honied phrase, all kind, pertinent to the occasion, and greatly fitted to strengthen, encourage and cheer."

When, about a month later, the first church-meeting was held in the Tabernacle and a record of thanks and gratitude to God was placed on the pages of the Church-book, Mrs. Spurgeon was the first of a long list of members to sign it after the names of the pastor, deacons and elders had been appended.

# CHAPTER VIII.

## HUSBAND AND WIFE.

MRS. SPURGEON, in the earlier years of her married life, used to accompany her husband in his holidays both in England and on the Continent, but in 1868, she tells us, her travelling days were done. " Henceforth for many years I was a prisoner in a sick - chamber, and my beloved had to leave me when the strain of his many labours and responsibilities compelled him to seek rest far away from home. These separations were very painful to hearts so tenderly united as were ours, but we each bore our share of the sorrow as heroically as we could and softened it as far as possible by constant correspondence." And what a delightful correspondence it was—love letters of the very best and highest kind.

"God bless you," wrote the husband on one occasion, "and help you to bear my absence. Better that I should be away well, than at home suffering—better to your loving heart, I know. Do not fancy, even for a moment, that absence could make our hearts colder to each other ; our attachment is now a perfect union, indissoluble for ever. My sense of your value and experience of your goodness are now united to the deep passion of love which was there at the first alone. Every year casts out another anchor to hold me even more firmly to you, though none was needed even from the first. May my own Lord, whose chastening hand has necessitated this absence, give you a secret inward recompense in soul and also another recompense in the healing of the body! All my heart remains in your keeping."

" Did I but know that you are better," he writes on another occasion, "I don't think I should have more to wish except your company," and a day or two later, " God be thanked for even the twinkling stars of better news in the letter I have just received from your dear self." In a letter from Rome, we find the passage: "I had two such precious letters from you this morning, worth to me far more than all the gems of ancient or modern art. The material of which they are composed is their main value, though there is also no mean skill revealed in its manipulation. They are pure as alabaster, far more precious than porphyry or verd antique; no mention shall be made of malachite or onyx, for love surpasses them all."

Charles Haddon Spurgeon looked upon

the writing of these letters as more than a
loving duty to his wife. Knowing how
pressed he was with other correspondence
that had to be attended to, and with
literary work, she often used to urge him
to write less often to her, so as to get more
rest for himself, but this he would not hear
of, and except when taking a long railway
journey, he used to write a letter to his
wife every day that he was absent from
her. "Every word I write," he says in
one note, "is a pleasure to me, as much as
ever it can be to you; it is only a lot of
odds and ends I send you, but I put them
down as they come, so that you may see
it costs me no labour, but is just a happy
scribble. Don't fret because I write you
so many letters; it is such a pleasure to
tell out my joy." At another time, when
sending some pen and ink sketches which
he had made of the women's head-dresses
in Italy, he writes, "Now, sweetheart, may
these trifles amuse you; *I count it a holy
work to draw them*, if they cause you but
one happy smile."

"That I smiled on them then, and weep
over them now," said Mrs. Spurgeon a year
or two ago, referring to these sketches
and the letter that accompanied them,
"is but a natural consequence of the
more complete separation which God has
willed for us,—he, dwelling in the land of

glory,—I, still tarrying amid the shadows of earth ;—but I verily believe that when I join him, 'beyond the smiling and the weeping,' there will be tender remembrances of all these details of earthly love and of the plenitudes of blessings which it garnered in our united lives. Surely we shall talk of all these things in the pauses of adoring worship and of joyful service. There must be sweet converse in Heaven between those who loved and suffered and served together here below. Next to the rapture of seeing the King in His beauty and beholding the face of Him who redeemed us to God by His blood, must be the happiness of the communion of saints in that place of inconceivable blessedness which God has prepared for them that love Him."

Those partings of husband and wife, after the latter became an invalid, must have been sore wrenches to Mrs. Spurgeon's heart, but in accordance with the resolution she had made before and at marriage, she never faltered, but gave her loved one up willingly for service or for those Continental holidays which were necessary for his health. " I thank God," she said late in life, "that he enabled me to carry out this determination and rejoice that I have no cause to reproach myself with being a drag on the swift wheels of his consecrated life. I do not take any credit to myself for this; it was the Lord's will concerning me, and He saw to it that I received the necessary training whereby in after years I could cheerfully surrender His chosen servant to the incessant demands of his ministry, his literary work, and the multiplied labours of his exceptionally busy life."

That this was no vain and empty boast was clearly confirmed by a letter which C. H. Spurgeon wrote to his wife in 1871, in which he declared, "None know how grateful I am to God for you. In all I have ever done for Him you have a large share, for in making me so happy you have fitted me for service. Not an ounce of power has ever been lost to the good cause through you. I have served the Lord far more and never less for your sweet companionship"

# CHAPTER IX.

## MIDDLE LIFE.

AFTER the preacher and his wife had been living in Helensburgh House, Nightingale Lane, for close upon a dozen years, the building was found altogether too small and inconvenient for a man whose work needed a very large library and consequently much space to store his books. The old house was loved for its happy associations by both husband and wife, but, realising the need for a more commodious dwelling, it was, after due consideration, decided to pull down the building and erect a new Helensburgh House which should meet the altered and increased needs of the preacher and his wife. The demolition took place in 1869, and on the site arose a handsome house with ample room for all the requirements of its owners. Mr. and Mrs. Spurgeon had always been lavishly generous with their money, and had at all times given every available pound that they possessed to one or other of the great causes which they had at heart. A few of their wealthier friends therefore came to the conclusion that it would be unfair to let them be saddled with the cost of the new house, which was only rendered a necessity because of the unselfish labours and extraordinary energy of the pastor in ever increasing his efforts for good, and these friends determined to defray the principal part of the cost as a token of their esteem and appreciation. Mr. William Higgs, the builder of the Metropolitan Tabernacle, built the new Helensburgh House, and no efforts were spared to make it a worthy gift and a suitable dwelling for the devoted minister and his invalid wife.

Some time before the building was ready for occupation, the preacher met the donors, and Mrs. Spurgeon, who had been staying at Brighton since the demolition of her old home, came up to London in order to be present at the gathering. C. H. Spurgeon made a dainty little speech, thanking his kind friends for their gift and paying a loving tribute to their generosity. "My wife and I," he concluded, "have firmly resolved that we will never go into debt for anything, yet you know something of the continuous claims upon us in connection with the work of the Lord," and he explained that the reason why he was not rich was that he refused to avail himself of many opportunities of acquiring wealth, such as by a lecturing trip to America, when he could have obtained

more money in a few weeks than he was
likely to receive through his ministry in
many years. "There is no intent on my
part to rest now that I have a new house.
If possible, I shall work harder than ever
before and preach better than ever," and
all that the speaker uttered for himself, he
declared, his wife re-echoed.

After this interesting meeting, Mrs.
Spurgeon, who was a great sufferer at the
period, went back to Brighton, where Sir
James Y. Simpson, of Edinburgh, performed a difficult operation upon her that
had the effect of giving her some relief
from pain and resulted in a slightly better
state of health. Meanwhile her husband
took upon himself the whole duty of
furnishing and preparing the new house
for habitation. How lovingly he did this
work, and how carefully he sought to please
his wife in all that he performed, the
following letter which Mrs. Spurgeon
received will show : —

"My Own Dear Sufferer,—I am pained
indeed to learn from T——'s kind note
that you are still in so sad a condition.
Oh, may the ever merciful God be pleased
to give you ease!

"I have been quite a long round to-day;
—if a 'round' can be 'long.' First to
Finsbury to buy the wardrobe,—a beauty.
I hope you will live long to hang your

garments in it, every thread of them precious to me for your dear sake. Next to Hewlett's for a chandelier for the dining-room. Found one quite to my taste and yours. Then to Negretti and Zambra's to buy a barometer for my own very fancy, for I have long promised to treat myself to one. On the road I obtained the Presburg biscuits, and within their box I send this note, hoping it may reach you the more quickly. They are sweetened with my love and prayers.

"The bedroom will look well with the wardrobe in it ; at least, so I hope. It is well made, and, I believe, as nearly as I could tell, precisely all you wished for. Joe [Mr. Joseph Passmore had given this as a present] is very good, and should have a wee note whenever darling feels she could write it without too much fatigue; but not yet. I bought also a table for you in case you should have to keep your bed. It rises or falls by a screw, and also winds side-ways, so as to go over the bed, and then it has a flap for a book or paper, so that my dear one may read or write in comfort while lying down. I could not resist the pleasure of making this little gift to my poor suffering wifey, only hoping it might not often be in requisition, but might be a help when there was a needs-be for it. Remember, all I buy, I pay for. I have

paid for everything as yet with the earnings
of my pen, graciously sent me in time of
need.    It is my ambition to leave nothing
for you to be anxious about.    I shall find
the money for the curtains, etc., and you
will amuse yourself by giving orders for
them after your own delightful taste.

"I must not write more; and, indeed,
matter runs short except the old, old story
of a love which grieves over you and would
fain work a miracle and raise you up to
perfect health.    I fear the heat afflicts you.
Well did the elder say to John in Patmos
concerning those who are before the throne
of God, 'Neither shall the sun light on
them nor any heat.'—Yours to love in life
and death, and eternally, C. H. S."

When everything was ready, Mrs. Spurgeon's health for a time forbade her
returning from Brighton, and her husband
had to inhabit the house alone.    But when
at last she could take up her abode once
again in Nightingale Lane she found that
the loving care of her husband had forgotten
nothing that could in any way conduce to
the comfort of an invalid almost entirely
confined to her couch.    "Never," she wrote,
"will the rapture with which he welcomed
her home be forgotten, nor the joyful pride
with which he pointed out all the arrange-
ments he had made so that her captivity
should have every possible compensation

and alleviation. There was a cunningly-contrived cupboard in one corner of the room into which he had gathered all the details of his loving care for her. When the doors were opened, a dainty washing apparatus was disclosed with hot and cold water laid on, so that no fatigue in ascending and descending the stairways should be necessary, and even the towels were embroidered with her name. He had thought of *everything;* and there were such tender touches of devoted love upon all the surroundings of the little room that no words can describe her emotions when first she gazed upon them, and afterwards when she proved by practical experience their exceeding usefulness and value."

During her sad illness at this time, Mrs. Spurgeon had one very remarkable instance of a desire of hers being granted by what cannot but be accepted as a Divine interposition. Her husband often used to ask if there were anything she would like him to get for her. The usual answer was a negative. But one day in a half-bantering tone she said, " I should like an opal ring and a piping bullfinch ! " Her husband was surprised, but replied, "Ah, you know I cannot get those for you! " For several days the curious request was laughed over, and then it passed from the memories of both husband and wife. Mrs. Spurgeon herself shall tell the sequel of the story. "One Thursday evening, on his return from the Tabernacle, he (the preacher) came into my room with such a beaming face and such love-lighted eyes, that I knew something had delighted him very much. In his hand he held a tiny box, and I am sure his pleasure exceeded mine as he took from it a beautiful little ring and placed it on my finger. 'There is your opal ring, my darling,' he said, and then he told me of the strange way in which it had come. An old lady, whom he had once seen when she was ill, sent a note to the Tabernacle to say she desired to give Mrs. Spurgeon a small present, and could someone be sent to her to receive it. Mr. Spurgeon's private secretary went accordingly and brought the little parcel, which, when opened, was found to contain this opal ring. How we talked of the Lord's tender love for His stricken child and of His condescension in thus stooping to supply an unnecessary gratification to His dear servant's sick one, I must leave my readers to imagine; but I can remember feeling that the Lord was very near to us.

"Not long after that I was moved to Brighton, there to pass a crisis in my life, the result of which would be a restoration to better health, or death. One evening, when my dear husband came from London, he brought a large package with him, and, uncovering it, disclosed a cage containing a lovely piping bullfinch! My astonishment was great, my joy unbounded, and these emotions were intensified as he related the way in which he became possessed of the coveted treasure. He had been to see a dear friend of ours, whose husband was sick unto death, and after commending the sufferer to God in prayer, Mrs. T—— said to him, 'I want you to take my pet bird to Mrs. Spurgeon; I would give him to none but her; his songs are too much for my poor husband in his weak state, and I know that "Bully" will interest and amuse Mrs. Spurgeon in her loneliness while you are so much away from her.' Mr. Spurgeon then told her of my desire for such a companion, and together they rejoiced over the care of the loving Heavenly Father, who had so wondrously provided the very gift His child had longed for. With that cage beside him the journey to Brighton was a very short one, and when 'Bully' piped his pretty song and took a hemp seed as a reward from the lips of his new mistress, there were eyes with joyful tears in them and hearts overflowing with praise to God in the little room by the sea that night, and the dear Pastor's comment was, 'I think you are one of your Heavenly Father's spoiled children, and He just gives you whatever you ask for.'

"Does anyone doubt that this bird was a direct love-gift from the pitiful Father?" asks Mrs. Spurgeon. "Do I hear someone say, 'Oh! it was all "chance" that brought about such coincidences as these'? Ah, dear friends, those of you who have been similarly indulged by Him *know* of a certainty that it is not so. He who cares for all the works of His hand cares with infinite tenderness for the children of His love, and thinks nothing which concerns them too small or too trivial to notice. If our faith were stronger and our love more perfect, we should see far greater marvels than these in our daily lives."

Although so weak and ailing and confined to her bedroom for such long periods of time, Mrs. Spurgeon was a faithful trainer of her twin sons in the Christian doctrine, and she had the joy of seeing them both brought to the Lord at an early age. "I trace my early conversion," Pastor Thomas Spurgeon has written, "directly to her earnest pleading and bright example. She denied herself the pleasure of attending Sunday evening services that she might minister the Word of Life to her household. There she taught me to sing, but to mean it first,—

> "'I do believe, I will believe,
>    That Jesus died for me;
> That, on the cross, He shed His blood
>    From sin to set me free.'

"My dear brother was brought to Christ through the pointed word of a missionary; but he, too, gladly owns that mother's influence and teaching had their part in the matter. By these, the soil was made ready for a later sowing." On September 21st, 1874, the sons were baptized by their father at the Metropolitan Tabernacle in the presence of an immense concourse of people, and Mrs. Spurgeon was herself an eye-witness of this open confession of faith made by her boys. On that occasion she was presented by the church with an illuminated address, in which hearty thanks were expressed " to Almighty God for calling so early in life to the fellowship of the saints the two sons of our beloved and honoured pastor," and praising "Our gracious Lord that it should have pleased Him to use so greatly the pious teachings and example of our dear sister, Mrs. Spurgeon, to the quickening and fostering of the Divine Life in the hearts of her twin sons, and we earnestly pray," concluded the address, "that amidst her long-continued sufferings she may ever be consoled with all spiritual comfort and by the growing devoutness of those who are thus twice given to her in the Lord."

# CHAPTER X.

## FOUNDING OF THE BOOK FUND.

MRS. SPURGEON, had she organised no new work herself, would always have been remembered as the wife of the great preacher, to whom she rendered such valuable help and encouragement, and who, to repeat C. H. Spurgeon's own words, was indeed as "an angel of God" to him. But, apart from any such associations and the reflected glory from her husband, Mrs. Spurgeon's name deserves to live for ever in the annals of the Christian Church in connection with her fund for supplying theological books to clergymen and ministers too poor to buy them. As a branch of Christian effort this work was, and is, quite unique, and its vast importance and necessity to the ministry and to the Church at large, cannot be over-estimated. In his preface to Mrs. Spurgeon's volume, "Ten Years of My Life in the Service of the Book Fund," the pastor of the Tabernacle expressed his conviction "that the work was sadly needed, has been exceedingly useful, and is still urgently called for." "How can many of our ministers buy books?" he

asked. " How can those in the villages
get them at all? What must their minis-
tries become if their minds are starved?
Is it not a duty to relieve the famine which
is raging in many a manse? Is it not a
prudential measure, worthy of the attention of all who wish to see the masses
influenced by religion, that the preachers
who occupy our pulpits should be kept
well furnished with material for thought?"
Incredible as it may seem, the state of
things revealed when the Book Fund was
started was so bad that many ministers
had been unable to buy a new book for ten
years. "Does anybody wonder if preachers
are sometimes dull?" was C. H. Spurgeon's
comment on this fact.

Like most other important works, the
Book Fund grew from a very simple
beginning, and there was no idea at the
first of the wonderful way in which the
movement would develop. In the summer
of 1875 Mr. Spurgeon completed the first
volume of his "Lectures to my Students,"
and, having given a proof copy to his wife,
asked her what she thought of the book.
"I wish I could place it in the hands of
every minister in England," was the reply,
and the preacher at once rejoined, "Then
why not do so: how much will you give?"
This was driving the nail home with a
vengeance. Mrs. Spurgeon was not pre-

pared for such a challenge, but she began
to wonder if she could not spare the money
from her housekeeping or personal account.
It would necessitate pressure somewhere,
she knew, for money was not plentiful just
then.   Suddenly a flash of memory made
the whole way clear.   "Upstairs in a little
drawer were some carefully hoarded crown
pieces, which, owing to some foolish fancy,
I had been gathering for years whenever
chance threw one in my way ; these I now
counted out and found they made a sum
*exactly* sufficient to pay for one hundred
copies of the work.   If a twinge of regret
at parting from my cherished but unwieldy
favourites passed over me, it was gone in
an instant, and then they were given
freely and thankfully to the Lord, and in
that moment, though I knew it not, the
Book Fund was inaugurated."

The next number of *The Sword and
the Trowel*, that for July, 1875, contained
an announcement of Mrs. Spurgeon's intention and inviting poor Baptist ministers to
apply for the book.   The applications proved
far more numerous than was anticipated, and
although she could not supply all demands,
the generous donor distributed two hundred
copies of the book instead of the one
hundred which she had at first proposed.
In *The Sword and the Trowel* for August,
C. H. Spurgeon referred to the matter

again and said, "It has been a great pleasure
to our beloved wife to give a book to so
many needy servants of the Lord ; but it
is a sad fact that there should be so many
needing such a present. Cannot something be done to provide ministers with
books? If they cannot be made rich in
money, they ought not for the people's
sake to be starved in soul." This appeal
had due effect, and friends began to forward money, so that by the following
month (September) parcels of books were
being sent out to ministers every day, and
the work was formally designated "Mrs.
Spurgeon's Book Fund." A gentleman
contributed a number of good books for
distribution among the poor ministers, and
other people, who were unable to send
money, followed his example and gave
volumes from their libraries. Of course,
the acceptance and acknowledgment of
gifts in kind led to a good deal of rubbish
being sent to Mrs. Spurgeon, who several
times had to gently protest against worth-
less volumes, fit only for the rag-shop, being
"presented " to the Book Fund. "I really
fear," she wrote in one report, "that some
people think that *anything in the shape
of a book* will do for a minister, or they
would scarcely send such things as ' Advice
to Mothers,' or ' Letters to a Son,' as aids
to pulpit preparation." On another occa-

sion she wrote : "There are in this pleasant world of ours many kind and tender-hearted people who, after perusing the report of my Book Fund, straightway rush off to their bookcases and in an enthusiasm of goodwill pull down a pile of old books and pack them off to me for my poor pastors, in the full belief that they have thus rendered the best possible service to the Fund and the Fund's Manager and the Fund's Manager's needy folk.   I should be very sorry to damp any kindly ardour or seem ungrateful for proofs of willing sympathy, but I feel constrained to point out as tenderly as possible to my well-meaning but mistaken friends that such presents are worse than useless to me.   I am often puzzled how to get rid of the encumbrances which were meant to be blessings!   Usually when good people thus disturb the dusty solitudes of their bookshelves the result is as follows:—A large number of volumes of *The Evangelical Magazine* and *The Baptist Record*, musty perhaps and always incomplete; some ancient 'Sermons' by the venerable pastor they 'sat under' half a century ago, a book or two of 'Poems' by 'nobody knows who,' a few old works on some abstruse notions, a 'French Grammar and Exercises,' Magnall's 'Questions,' 'Advice to a Newly Married Pair,' and—I was going to say—a 'Cookery Book,' but I think that might be an exaggeration where all else is simple, earnest fact. Now, what could my poor pastors care for rubbish such as this?" C. H. Spurgeon himself, in acknowledging in his magazine the first gift of valuable books from the gentleman above-mentioned, said, "We have on several occasions in days past received parcels consisting of old magazines and the sweepings of libraries, and we have concluded that the donors thought we kept a butter shop, but this friend has sent really standard volumes, which will, we trust, be a boon to some poor preacher."

During the autumn Mrs. Spurgeon became seriously ill and the distribution of books had to be delayed, but by November she had sufficiently recovered to commence work again, and scarcely a day went by but what some poor minister was made happy by receiving a gift of volumes which his slender means would never have allowed him to purchase. No distinction as to denomination was made, and although the poverty of Baptist ministers was perhaps more acute than that of others, yet there were hundreds of preachers in all the Churches quite unable to purchase the books which they absolutely needed for their work. It was not long before the valuable volumes of "The Treasury of

David" were added to the "Lectures," and gradually other books were distributed, mostly C. H. Spurgeon's own writings and sermons, as these were generally asked for by the poor ministers applying. By January, 1876, without any solicitation, friends had sent in £182, and this had increased in August, one year after the inauguration of the Fund, to upwards of £500, representing a distribution of 3,058 volumes. By a generous arrangement of the publishers of C. H. Spurgeon's works, the books were supplied for purposes of the Fund at a very low rate, so that £500 in money would purchase about £800 worth of books.

The novel and important work was now established on a solid and permanent basis, and the interest in the movement to furnish poor ministers' libraries was increasing.

Quoting from the letters of recipients, who expressed their intense joy and thankfulness at receiving the books, Mrs. Spurgeon wrote in *The Sword and the Trowel* after the first twelve months' work : "Now this is very beautiful and admirable, but is there not also something most sorrowfully suggestive to the Church of God ? Surely these 'servants of Christ,' these 'ambassadors for God,' ought to have received better treatment at our hands than to have been left pining so long without the aids

which are vitally necessary to them in their
sacred calling. Books are as truly a
minister's needful tools as the plane and
the hammer and the saw are the necessary
adjuncts of a carpenter's bench. We pity
a poor mechanic, whom accident has
deprived of his working gear, we straightway get up a subscription to restore it, and
certainly never expect a stroke of work
from him while it is lacking; why, I
wonder, do we not bring the same common-
sense help to our poor ministers, and
furnish them liberally with the means of
procuring the essentially important books?
Is it not pitiful to think of their struggling
on from year to year on £100, £80, £60,
and some (I am ashamed to write it) on less
than £50 per annum? Many have large
families, many more sick wives, some, alas!
have both; they have heavy doctors' bills
to pay, their children's education to provide
for, are obliged to keep up a respectable
appearance, or their hearers would be
scandalized; and how they manage to do
all this and yet keep out of debt (as, to
their honour and credit be it said, the
majority of them do), only they and their
ever-faithful God can know! I never hear
a word of complaint from them, only sometimes a pathetic line or two like this:
' After upwards of sixteen years' service
in the Master's vineyard I am sorry to say

that, with a small salary and a wife and
five daughters to provide for, my library is
exceedingly small, and I am not in a position to increase its size by purchasing
books.' Or, again, like this: 'My salary
is small (£60), and if I did not get some
little help from some benevolent societies, I
should have very great difficulty in keeping
the wolf from the door.' Are these men to
be kept in poverty so deep that they posi-
tively cannot afford the price of a new
book without letting their little ones go
barefoot? 'The labourer is worthy of his
hire,' but these poor labourers in the gospel
field get a pittance which is unworthy both
of the workman and the work, and if their
people (who ought to help them more)
either cannot or will not do so, we at least,
dear friends, will do all in our power to
encourage their hearts and refresh their
drooping spirits. This is a digression, I
daresay from my authorized subject, but I
was obliged to say what I have said,
because my heart was hot within me, and
I so earnestly want to do these poor
brethren good service."

Mrs. Spurgeon took as her motto the
words which her husband put into the
mouth of the spendthrift in "John Ploughman's Talk." "Spend and God will send,"
and before the Book Fund was nine months
old she had a remarkable proof of her faith

being honoured. A gentleman sent £50 for the Fund, the largest gift received up to that time, and it was quickly distributed in the form of books. About six months later the same gentleman (who insisted upon remaining anonymous to everyone else) called upon Mrs. Spurgeon and declared his intention of giving to every one of the five hundred Calvinistic Methodist ministers, preachers and students in North Wales, through the Book Fund, a copy of " Lectures to My Students," and at the same time he handed over another sum of £50 to meet expenses. Before the distribution in North Wales was completed, the same generous donor gave authority to Mrs. Spurgeon to continue at his expense the despatch of copies to the ministers and preachers in South Wales.

# CHAPTER XI.

## THE BOOK FUND GROWS.

A FEW months before the Book Fund originated, Mrs. Spurgeon had sown in a large garden flower-pot some lemon pips, hoping that one at least of them would spring up and grow into a healthy plant. Sure enough, one did take root, and a frail stem with two tiny leaves made its appearance, and was tenderly cared for by its owner. In a happy moment Mrs. Spurgeon's mind associated her Book Fund, then a "tender plant," whose continued existence might be precarious, but which had splendid possibilities in it, with the little lemon tree, and as the latter flourished and increased, she determined to regard it as something in the nature of an augury of the prosperity of her Fund, each leaf representing a sum of a hundred pounds, which sooner or later would surely come to hand. The growth of the tree was steady and continuous, and, curiously enough, the Fund kept pace with it. As fresh leaves were formed, so new subscribers came forward to help on Mrs. Spurgeon's labour of love, and all through their history the Book Fund and the lemon tree were associated in the mind of the lady, to whom they were both so dear.

Although subscriptions were not solicited, there was no lack of funds. Between August, 1876, and January, 1877, no less than £926 was received, and by the end of the second year more than £2,000 had come in and been expended. The progress of time only served to show how widespread was the need, and the letters which Mrs. Spurgeon received by the score each week formed pathetic reading, whilst the gratitude expressed by recipients of books was quite painful in its intensity.

She had been trained in her husband's school of faith, and it was to God and not to man that she looked both for the money to carry on her mission and for the health and strength to enable her to cope with the ever growing work of correspondence and organization. "The Book Fund has been nourished and fed from the King's Treasury," she wrote in 1877, " and I must 'make my boast in the Lord' that all needful supplies for the carrying on of the work have plainly borne the stamp of Heaven's own merit. I say this because I have never asked help of anyone but Him, never solicited a donation from any creature, yet money has always been forthcoming and the supplies have constantly been in due proportion to the needs.

Once only during the year did the Lord try my faith by allowing the grants of books to outnumber the gifts of money, and then it was only for a 'small moment' that a fear overshadowed me. The dark cloud very speedily passed away, and fresh supplies made me more than ever satisfied with the resolution I had formed to draw only on the unlimited resources of my heavenly Treasurer. None of the friends whose hearts have 'devised liberal things' on behalf of my work will reproach me with ingratitude towards them when I lay my *first* loving thanks at His feet; they will rather join me in praising Him for so sweetly inclining their hearts to help His needy ones, and will joyfully say, 'O Lord, of Thine own have we given thee.'

"I recall with very glad satisfaction the first donation which reached me 'for sending books to ministers.' It came anonymously, and was but five shillings' worth of stamps, yet it was very precious and proved like a revelation to me, for it opened up a vista of possible usefulness and exceeding brightness. The mustard seed of my faith grew forthwith into a 'great' tree, and sweet birds of hope and expectation sat singing in its branches. 'You'll see,' I said to my boys, 'the Lord will send me hundreds of pounds for this work.' For many a day afterwards mother's 'hundreds of pounds' became a 'household word' of good-humoured merriment and badinage. And now 'the Lord has made me to laugh,' for the hundreds have grown into thousands. He has done 'exceeding abundantly above what I could ask or even think,' and faith, with such a God to believe in and depend upon, ought surely to smile at impossibilities and say 'it shall be done.'"

The work which Mrs. Spurgeon had undertaken did not for very long confine itself exclusively to the supply of books. At the beginning of 1877 a friend placed at her disposal a sum of money from which she could draw such amounts as were necessary for the relief of poor ministers in dire financial straits, and, her husband and other friends adding to this sum, a very useful and much-needed Pastors' Aid Fund was founded, which has proved a valuable auxiliary and supplement to the Book Fund. At the end of the year, too, a number of Christian ladies undertook to supply warm garments and other suitable clothing for the families of poor pastors, and this branch of the work has also gone on increasing to the present time. Still another advance was made when two friends provided the means for sending *The Sword and the Trowel* regularly for a year to each of sixty ministers who could not afford to purchase a religious magazine for themselves. Perhaps these developments of Mrs. Spurgeon's original idea were foreshadowed by the announcement which the gardener made to her some time earlier: "Your lemon tree is brought up to the house, ma'am. It is making a great deal of new wood."

In 1878, Mrs. Spurgeon's malady reached an acute stage, and indeed so serious was her condition that her son Thomas, who was then in Australia, received an urgent cable to return at once. For some time her life was despaired of, but the crisis was passed successfully, and, although still an invalid, she was able once again to give all her attention to the Book Fund. The work, however, did not diminish on account of the illness, for the arrears were soon made up and the year was the most successful since the inauguration. Those periods of pain and weariness, which Mrs. Spurgeon was called upon to suffer, never led her to despair or to rebel against the strange providence that had so marked out a hilly path for her. If for a moment the mystery of life perplexed her, she quickly found comfort and consolation by trusting to Him who doeth all things well. Her diaries or note-books contain many entries which tell of her experiences of soul during the most trying periods of her life.

Referring to this time of crisis she writes :

"At the close of a very dark and gloomy day I lay resting on my couch as the deeper night drew on, and though all was bright within my cosy little room, some of the external darkness seemed to have entered into my soul and obscured its spiritual vision. Vainly I tried to see the hand which I knew held mine and guided my fog-enveloped feet along a steep and slippery path of suffering. In sorrow of heart I asked, ' Why does my Lord thus deal with His child ? Why does he so often send sharp and bitter pain to visit me ? Why does he permit lingering weakness to hinder the sweet service I long to render to His poor servants ? ' These fretful questions were quickly answered, and though in a strange language, no interpreter was needed save the conscious whisper of my own heart.

"For a while silence reigned in the little room, broken only by the crackling of an oak log burning on the hearth. Suddenly I heard a sweet, soft sound, a little, clear, musical note, like the tender trill of a robin beneath my window. ' What *can* it be ? ' I said to my companion, who was dozing in the firelight ; ' surely no bird can be singing out there at this time of the year and night ! ' We listened, and again heard the faint

plaintive notes, so sweet, so melodious, yet
mysterious enough to provoke for a
moment our undisguised wonder.  Presently my friend exclaimed, ' It comes from
the log on the fire!' and we soon ascer-
tained that her surprised assertion was
correct.   The fire was letting loose the imprisoned music from the old oak's inmost
heart.  Perchance he had garnered up this
song in the days when all went well with
him, when birds twittered merrily on his
branches, and the soft sunlight flecked his
tender leaves with gold ; but he had grown
old since then and hardened ; ring after
ring of knotty growth had sealed up the
long-forgotten melody until the fierce
tongues of the flames came to consume his
callousness and the vehement heat of the
fire wrung from him at once a song and a
sacrifice.

"Oh! thought I, when the fire of
affliction draws songs of praise from us,
then indeed are we purified and our God
is glorified!  Perhaps some of us are like
this old oak log—cold, hard and insensible ;
we should give forth no melodious sounds
were it not for the *fire* which kindles
round us, and releases tender notes of trust
in Him, and cheerful compliance with His
will.   As I mused the fire burned and my
soul found sweet comfort in the parable so
strangely set forth before me.   Singing in

the fire! Yes, God helping us if that is the only way to get harmony out of these hard, apathetic hearts, let the furnace be heated seven times hotter than before." How the suffering wife had caught the spirit and faith of her husband, who, in *his* sufferings, later on, wrote words almost to the same effect as the foregoing!

The story of the Book Fund in its financial department during these early days, and indeed up till the present, is very much like that of the Stockwell Orphanage or the Pastors' College, on a small scale. Unsolicited the money would come in from the most unexpected sources just when it was needed, and would be spent without delay in the full and faithful expectation that more would follow to take its place. An entry in Mrs. Spurgeon's note-book a month or two after that which records the message of the burning oak log says, "My heart praises and extols the goodness of the Lord, and my hand shall at once record the mercy which, like a blessed rain on a thirsty land, has so sweetly refreshed my spirit. This afternoon a constant and generous friend brought £100 for the Book Fund. This was cause for devout thankfulness and great joy, for lately an unusually large number of books has been going out week by week though funds have flowed in less freely. But it was not

till a few hours after receiving this noble
donation that I saw fully the Lord's tender
care and pitying love in sending me this
help *just when* he knew I should most
sorely need it. By the late post that
night came my quarterly account for
books, and so heavy was it, that in fear
and haste I turned to my ledger to see the
available balance, and with an emotion I
shall not easily forget, I found that, but
for the gift of £100 a few hours previously,
I should have been £60 in debt. Did not
the Father's care thus keep the sparrow
from falling to the ground? A sleepless
night and much distress of spirit would
have resulted from my discovery of so
serious a deficit in my funds, but the Lord's
watchful love prevented this. 'Before I
called He answered,' and though trouble
was not very distant, He had said, 'It
shall not come nigh thee.' O my soul,
bless thou the Lord and forget not this
His loving ' benefit ' ! A tumult of joy and
delight arose within me as I saw in this
incident, not a mere chance or a happy
combination of circumstances, but the
guiding and sustaining hand of the loving
Lord, who had most certainly arranged
and ordered for me this pleasant way of
comfort and relief. ' I am poor and needy,
yet the Lord thinketh upon me.' A fresh
revelation of His wonderful love seemeth

to be vouchsafed to my soul by this opportune blessing and a cheque became ' an outward and visible sign of an inward and spiritual grace.'

" I hastened to my dear husband that he might share my joy, and I found in him a willing listener to the sweet 'old story' of his Master's grace and power. Then, after a word or two of fervent praise to God on my behalf, he wrote the following letter to the friend by whose liberal hand our gracious God had sent this notable deliverance :—' Dear friend,—I should like you to know why you were sent here this afternoon, and what an angel of mercy you were to my dear wife and so to me. The Lord bless you. Soon after you were gone my wife's quarter's bill for books came in for £340, and she had only £280 apart from your cheque. Poor soul! she has never spent more than her income before, and if you had not come, I fear it would have crushed her to be £60 in debt. How good of the Lord to send you in the nick of time! We joined our praises together, and we do also very gratefully join our prayers for you. God bless you, and make up to you your generous gifts above all your own desires. I could not refrain from telling you this; it is one of the sparkling facts which will make happy memories to help to stay our faith in future trials if they come again. God bless you.—Yours heartily, C. H. SPURGEON.' "

Exactly a week after the above entry in Mrs. Spurgeon's diary we find another of similar purport. " £20 from a *new* friend to-day! My heart keeps whispering, 'Indulgent God, how kind!' At the beginning of this week I had hesitated about sending my usual order for books, having less in hand than would justify a large increase of stock, but I ventured, and lo! the Lord has sent me all I need for present wants, and with it a firm assurance to my soul that 'those who trust in Him shall never be ashamed.' "

Money now began to be received in considerable sums. Gifts of twenty-five and fifty pounds from single individuals were by no means uncommon, and from the great Silver Wedding Testimonial presented by the Tabernacle Church to C. H. Spurgeon the Book Fund received £100, and the Pastors' Aid Fund another £100.

Of course there were disappointments, but the trials only increased the faith. Thus after losing an expected bequest of £200, Mrs. Spurgeon wrote : "A legacy of £200 left to the Book Fund by an old and much loved friend becomes null and void in consequence of legal inaccuracies in the will ; and thus, though the dear deceased's tender remembrance of me is inalienable, I lose the splendid help to my beloved work which she intended should partly alleviate my grief at her departure and in some measure compensate for the cessation of her constant loving aid. I try to bear my disappointment bravely and sink my own sorrow in sympathy with the President in the far heavier loss sustained in like manner by the Pastors' College, and though I felt at first to some extent 'bowed down' by the unexpected failure of my promised good fortune, I am since upholden and comforted exceedingly, for I know that 'the Lord is able to give me much more than this,' and this puts all thought of murmuring from me, and enables me to look up again from human help to that infinitely more certain portion with which the Lord supplies all my need as it arises. Perhaps I needed such a lesson, and shall do well to learn it off 'by heart.' It is quite possible that I felt too elated on hearing of the generous bequest and counted up my riches with somewhat of carnal pride mingling with the gratification which was allowable; certain it is that I once reckoned upon a grand total at the end of the year quite eclipsing all former amounts, and it may be that the Lord saw this was not good for me, and that the reception of too much 'treasure laid up on earth' would have disturbed and imperilled that lovely posture of constant dependence on my God which He has taught me to delight in, and has so graciously honoured and rewarded. I think also I may learn from this untoward event to bless and praise Him more humbly and heartily for His grand and immutable 'Will' and that 'His ways are not our ways.'"

After her own comparative recovery in 1879 Mrs. Spurgeon's husband fell ill, and had to go to the South of France, whence frequent bulletins were cabled, giving news of his condition to the anxious wife at home. The work of the Book Fund, however, kept her from brooding over her sorrow. A note-book entry in December says, " Blessed be God! Better news comes now. The telegrams have ceased and letters written with unsteady pen by poor pained hands, yet inexpressibly precious, have arrived. In this trying time hard work has been a benefactor to me, for the urgency of the daily correspondence admits of no comfortable nursing of grief, and Book Fund management knows no cessation while the Lord sends so many needy applicants."

The gifts were not confined to poor preachers in Great Britain, although naturally the majority of parcels were distributed in the homeland. But many a missionary has been helped in his work by a grant from the Book Fund, and native preachers in the West Indies, Africa, and elsewhere, have participated in the benefits of the Fund. In June, 1879, the Bishop of Sierra Leone, Dr. Cheetham, who had heard of the good work which Mrs. Spurgeon had instituted and was carrying on, called upon her at Helensburgh House and solicited the gift of " The Treasury of David " for one of his coloured pastors. Mrs. Spurgeon readily promised to give these books, and also some others, and the Bishop before he left enrolled his name as a donor to the Fund. In Jamaica the gifts of books were greatly appreciated by both the English missionaries and the native pastors.

# CHAPTER XII.

## CONTINUED SUCCESS OF THE BOOK FUND.

TO give anything like a history of Mrs. Spurgeon's Book Fund in these pages is quite out of the question. Those who wish for a detailed account of how the work grew and thrived and developed year after year will find it in the volumes of reports which Mrs. Spurgeon herself prepared, "Ten Years of My Life" and "Ten Years After." That the work did grow and did thrive and did develop a comparison of the statistics for succeeding twelvemonths will clearly show. Thus in 1881 the number of volumes distributed was 7,298, and 10,517 single sermons by C. H. Spurgeon were sent off in parcels for free distribution. In 1883 the books for the year had increased to 11,351; in the following year the number stood at 9,149 and the sermons at 11,981, whilst three years later the annual distribution included 10,311 volumes and 21,227 sermons. The numbers have varied in the different years since that time according to the state of the finances, and owing to the growing infirmity of Mrs. Spurgeon the work has receded somewhat from its high-water mark of 1883. The last report issued by her, that for the years 1901 and 1902, showed that 10,113 volumes had been distributed during the two years, and that in the twenty-seven years since the Fund was started a total of 199,315 valuable theological works had been put into the hands of ministers, preachers and missionaries too poor to purchase them. It is indeed a marvellous record of service done by an invalid lady, and to find a parallel would be difficult. The whole of the work entailed by the Book Fund and its branch organizations was attended to by Mrs. Spurgeon personally, and some idea of how heavy was the correspondence alone, may be gathered from the fact that the average number of letters received per month was about five hundred, and in two periods of four weeks each the numbers were 657 and 755 respectively. Nor was the work all composed of "pleasant fruit and flowers," for, as Mrs. Spurgeon tells us, in referring to the fact that her lemon tree had developed a few sharp thorns, there were in connection with the Book Fund "some thorns concealed here and there which wound the hand that inadvertently touches them." Some ministers, whose behaviour showed either that they greatly misunderstood the nature of the Book Fund or that

their characters were strangely out of keeping with their office, would write in such a
strain as practically amounted to a demand
for books whilst others quite ignored the
conditions on which the volumes were given
and loftily declined to say whether their
incomes were under the £150 per annum,
which was laid down as the limit.   One
man, who had requested a grant without
saying anything as to his financial condition, when asked kindly whether his income
brought him within the sphere of the work,
replied angrily, "Permit me to say I have
no wish to be considered a *pauper.*"

"Ever since the Master gave me this
charge to keep," wrote Mrs. Spurgeon when
mentioning the above incident, "He knows
I have tried to minister in gentle, kindly
fashion to His servants, but occasionally
the spirit of my service is overlooked by
them, and my gifts are either claimed as a
right or disdained as a charity.   Few and
far between are these ugly thorns on my
beautiful tree ; tender and loving acknow-
ledgments of my work are the rule and
when an exception comes I can well afford
to forgive and forget it.   Were it not that
a chronicler is required to be faithful and
give fairly both sides of the history he is
writing, I should have left unrecorded this
painful part of a most pleasant and blessed
service."

It is truly wonderful that being so often prostrated, Mrs. Spurgeon was able to keep the Book Fund in so flourishing a condition. Over and over again she was completely laid aside, and when once more convalescent her weakness was such that none but a woman whose whole being was given up to service for the Lord could have sustained the mental and physical stress of such a great work. In his preface to "Ten Years of My Life," the substantial profits from which, owing to the generosity of the authoress and publishers, were given to the Book Fund, C. H. Spurgeon wrote : "I gratefully adore the goodness of our Heavenly Father in directing my beloved wife to a work which has been, to her, fruitful in unutterable happiness. That it has cost her more pain than it would be fitting to reveal is most true ; but that it has brought her a bound-less joy is equally certain. Our gracious Lord ministered to His suffering child in the most effectual manner when He graciously led her to minister to the neces-sities of His servants. By this means He called her away from her personal griefs, gave tone and concentration to her life, led her to continual dealings with Himself, and raised her nearer the centre of that region where other than earthly joys and sorrows reign supreme. Let every believer accept this as the inference of experience : that for most human maladies the best relief and antidote will be found in self-sacrificing work for the Lord Jesus."

The writer went on, however, to say that his wife's increasing weakness was not equal to continuing the work at its present increasing rate. "From this date the beloved worker feels that she must slacken. The business has overpowered her : the waggon is running over the horse. A measure of this ministry *must* pass into other hands, for, to my great sorrow, I have seen that overpressure is now causing a growing sense of weariness. It cannot long be possible to wake up every morning with a dread of that pile of letters ; to sit all day with scarce an interval, writing and book-keeping ; and to go to bed at night with a sigh that the last stroke has hardly been made before the eyes have closed. However brave an invalid may be, love will not always allow such incessant toil to grind down a willing spirit. As the embodiment of loving prudence I feel that I must place an urgent veto upon the continuance of this labour *at its present rate.*"

But although there was a slight diminution in the work, Mrs. Spurgeon remained at her post, and with the exception of one period in the year 1888, when she was so seriously ill that her severe physical suffering deprived her of all ability to continue her labours or even to open her letters, she carried on the Book Fund to the end of her life. Often the persistent and steady labour taxed her energy to its utmost limit, but the work was done and done well. No distinction as to church or creed was made in the distribution of books, and among the 25,000 or more ministers who have benefited by the Fund up to the present time are those belonging to the Church of England, the Baptists, the Congregationalists, all kinds of Methodists, the Presbyterians, the Moravians, the Society of Friends, the Unitarians, the Irvingites, the Waldensians, the Nestorians, the Plymouth Brethren, the Lutherans, the Swedenborgians, the Countess of Huntingdon's Connexion, and the Morrisonians, besides a very large number of evangelists and missionaries.

In the earlier days of the Fund's history it was always a grief to Mrs. Spurgeon that she was unable to accede to the pathetic requests for books made by poor local preachers, as the applications from regular ministers were more than sufficient to absorb all her grants. She mentioned this matter in her report for 1887, and, after quoting from a letter, said : "This is a real cry for help ; will it not touch the heart of any who can respond to it ? " The appeal did touch the heart of a willing worker, Mr. Sydney S. Bagster, of the Conference Hall, Mildmay Park, who organized a successful Auxiliary Book Fund for the free distribution of theological works among poor lay preachers. The work of sending off parcels commenced on May 1st, 1888, and by the end of that year 126 preachers had received 1,142 volumes. Mr. Bagster continued to carry on the Auxiliary Book Fund until 1891, when it was handed over to Mrs. Spurgeon, and became a part of the regular work carried on at her home. On an average about sixteen hundred volumes have been distributed annually among the poor local preachers up to the present time.

As year followed year there were increasing developments, which added to the labours of the devoted founder of the Book Fund. The monthly grant of copies of *The Sword and the Trowel*, already referred to, assumed large proportions. Many thousands of C. H. Spurgeon's sermons and other pamphlets were sent out each year to preachers both at home and abroad, and there has been for a long time past a Fund for General Use in the Work of the Lord which bore the expense of the translation of C. H. Spurgeon's sermons into foreign languages and their publication, as well as supplying help to preachers and others in need, to chapels handicapped by a debt, and various missions needing monetary assistance.

The Pastors' Aid Fund became an established institution, and each year Mrs. Spurgeon was able to distribute an average of over three hundred pounds among the pastors and their families who had needs more pressing than ordinary. The grants of bonnets, shawls, and other articles of clothing has also been an important offshoot and auxiliary of the Book Fund.

Up to the last Mrs. Spurgeon regarded her lemon tree with a rare affection as being a remarkable symbol of her work. At the conclusion of the volume, "Ten Years After," she wrote : "The great central stem is, metaphorically, *The Book Fund* itself, out of which all the branches have naturally grown, and with which they all continue to be vitally connected. Springing from the main trunk, and almost rivalling it in strength and usefulness, is the largest limb of the tree, which represents *The Pastors' Aid Fund.* This, in its turn, has thrown out the widely-spreading branch from which the well-filled boxes of *The 'Westwood' Clothing Society* have dropped into many a poor pastor's home. Peering between the thickly-interlaced foliage I spy a sturdy bough bearing the inscription *Home Distribution of Sermons,* and an equally vigorous offshoot dedicated

to *The Circulation of the Sermons Abroad*,
while the topmost twigs, on which *I* can
plainly read the words *Foreign Trans-
lations of Sermons*, bid fair to rival in all
respects their older companions.    To me,
*their* rapid growth is most cheering, for
their leaves contain so much of the essential oil of ' the Tree of Life ' that they are
in a very literal sense ' for the healing of
the nations.'   One shoot of the lemon tree,
which drooped awhile, but now flourishes
as freely as the other branches, symbolizes
*The    Auxiliary    Book    Fund ;*    another
reminds me of *The Sword and Trowel
distribution*, while the many thousands of
*tracts and pamphlets* which are circulated
by the Fund are well represented by the
twigs and leaves which spring from the
larger stems."

All through, Mrs. Spurgeon was herself
a most generous donor to the Book Fund
finances, her personal services being supple-
mented by monetary gifts far greater than
is generally supposed ; while by her will
the Fund benefits to a considerable extent.

# CHAPTER XIII.

## LAST YEARS OF MARRIED LIFE.

IN 1880 Mr. and Mrs. Spurgeon removed from Nightingale Lane, Clapham, to "Westwood," Beulah Hill, Norwood, their last home on earth. The remarkable circumstances attending the sale of the old house and the purchase of the new have been told fully in "The Life of Charles Haddon Spurgeon," and it is unnecessary to repeat the story here. The new home was a great improvement on the old; not only was it situated farther from the smoke and noise of London, but the rooms were much more ample and convenient than those of Helensburgh House, and the grounds covered nearly nine acres. The actual changing, however, was a time of much discomfort, although Mrs. Spurgeon's health was far better than it had been for a long time past.

"What a stirring up of one's quiet nest this removal is," she wrote in her diary, "and how tenderly one learns to look on familiar objects from which we are to be parted for ever. The heart yearns over a place endeared by an intimate acquaintance of twenty-three years and full of

happy and solemn associations. Every
nook and corner, both of house and garden,
abounds with sweet or sorrowful memories,
and the remembrance of manifold mercies
cling like a rich tapestry to the walls of the
desolate rooms. On this spot nearly a
quarter of a century of blissful wedded life
has been passed, and though both husband
and wife have been called to suffer severe
physical pain and months of weakness
within its boundary, our house has been far
oftener a 'Bethel' to us than a 'Bochim.'
The very walls might cry out against us as
ungrateful did we not silence them by our
ceaseless thanksgiving, for the Lord has
here loaded us with benefits and consecrated every inch of space with tokens of
His great lovingkindness. The sun of His
goodness has photographed every portion
of our dear home upon our hearts, and
though other lights and shadows must be
reflected there in coming days, they can
never obliterate the sweet images which
grateful memory will jealously preserve.
Tender remembrance will render indelible
the pictures of the sick chamber—which so
many times had almost been 'the gate of
heaven' to our spirit; the little room, tenderly fitted up by a husband's careful love,
and so often the scene of a scarcely hoped-
for convalescence; the study—sacred to
the Pastor's earnest work and silent witness

of wrestlings and communings known only to God and his own soul; the library— where the shelves gladly suffered a constant spoliation and renewal for the blessed work of the Book Fund.

"It is hard to leave all these sympathetic surroundings and dwell in the house of a stranger, but we believe we have seen the cloudy pillar move, and heard our Leader's voice bidding us 'go forward,' so in trustful obedience we strike our tent and prepare to depart to the 'place of which He has told us.' And our new home may be to us a 'Tabor' if our Lord will but dwell with us there."

After the removal, Mrs. Spurgeon was delighted with her new home. "In spite of the turmoil and trouble caused by the painful process of removal," she writes, "our first fortnight on Beulah's Hill has been a time of great and unaccustomed joy. Blest for this period with a singular accession of health and strength, the new owners together visited the various spots of interest in their little kingdom, making pleasant discoveries every day; now tracing a winding garden path to some unexpected opening, now looking with growing admiration upon the glorious views of earth and sky, ever breathing the bright, clear air with a lively sense of exhilaration and refreshment, and constantly pausing to marvel at the goodness of God in ' choosing such an inheritance for them.' It seems almost like living a new life, and as if pain and sickness were left behind in the valley for ever. . . . . These bright days and golden hours may not last long, but they are very precious in present possession, and will leave blissful memories behind them."

On Saturdays, here, as in their other homes, husband and wife would work together in the preparation of the sermon which the former was to deliver on the coming morning, and happy indeed were the times thus spent. Sometimes when the preacher had been unable to settle upon a text, he would say, "Wifey, what shall I do? God has not given me a text yet," and Mrs. Spurgeon would comfort him as well as she could. Perhaps she would be able to suggest a suitable passage, in which case her husband, after preaching, would give her due credit in referring to the sermon by saying: " You gave me that text." When the lady was called into the study on these Saturday evenings by her husband there was always an easy chair, she tells us, drawn up to the table by Mr. Spurgeon's side, and a number of open books piled one upon another from which she used to read as directed by her husband. "With these old volumes around him he was like a honey-bee amid the flowers; he seemed to know how to extract and carry off the sweet spoils from the most unpromising-looking tome among them. His acquaintance with them was so familiar and complete that he could at once place his hand on any author who had written upon the portion of Scripture which was engaging his attention ; and I was, in this pleasant fashion, introduced to many of the Puritan and other divines, whom otherwise I might not have known."

The change to Norwood, it was anticipated, might be of benefit to C. H. Spurgeon's health, and render unnecessary those annual winterings at Mentone. But this did not prove to be the case. His painful ailment continued, and the sad partings of husband and wife had to go on year after year, he thinking of her in the lonely house in England, she full of anxiety for the loved one away on the Riviera, whose agony from the gout was oftentimes beyond endurance. But even then his letters to his wife were full of humour, so as to cheer her and make things seem as bright as possible. "I feel as if I were emerging from a volcano," he once wrote at the commencement of a convalescence, and on the notepaper he had sketched a hill from the crater of which his head and shoulders were rising.

As time went on the preacher's illnesses

became longer, and the painfulness of his malady more acute. In November, 1890, he went to Mentone full of hope, and on arriving wrote to Mrs. Spurgeon: "What heavenly sunshine! This is like another world. I cannot quite believe myself to be on the same planet. God grant that this may set me all right! Only three other visitors in the hotel—three American ladies —*room for you.*" But the next day the dreadful gout attacked the patient's right hand and arm. Even then he wrote: "The day is like one in Eden before our first parents fell. When my head is better I shall enjoy it. I have *eau de Cologne* dripped on to my hot brain-box; and as I have nothing to do but to look out on the perfect scene before me, my case is not a bad one." The attack, however, increased in virulence, and for eight days he was unable himself to write to Mrs. Spurgeon; but he sent a message through his private secretary: "Give her my love, and say I am very bad, and I wish I were at home for her to nurse me; but as I am not, I shall be helped through somehow." Then came a letter, almost unreadable, so difficult a task had the tracing of the characters been: "Beloved, to lose right hand is to be dumb. I am better except at night. Could not love his darling more. Wished myself at home when pains came, but when worst this soft

clear air helps me. It is as heaven's gate.
All is well. Thus have I stammered a line
or two. Not quite dumb, bless the Lord!
What a good Lord He is! I shall yet
praise Him. Sleeplessness cannot so
embitter the night as to make me fear when
He is near." The letter was signed, "Your
own beloved *Benjamite*"—a humorous
reference to the fact that it had been
written with the left hand. After this, progress was slow, but such expressions as,
"Oh, that you were here!" clearly show
how he longed to have his wife by his side.
On December 8th he wrote, gleefully :
"To-day I dressed myself," and concluded,
"You write so sweetly. Yours is a hand
which sets to music all it writes to me. God
bless you! But you don't say how you are.
If you do not, I will write every day." Mrs.
Spurgeon had lovingly sought to conceal
her own weakness, so as not to give any
additional pain to her husband. When the
English winter proved to be very cold, he
wrote : "Poor darling to be so cold. The
Lord will soon hear prayer and send the
soft South wind upon you, and then I also
shall get well, and go out for walks and
praise His Name. I wish I could think of
something to cast a gleam of sunlight over
' Westwood.' If my love were light you
would live in the sun. I shall send you
some roses to-morrow, and they will

prophesy of better days," and a few days
later : "I keep on praying for change of
weather for you and the poor and sick.  I
wish I could send you a brazier of the coals
of my heart, which have a most vehement
flame."

Such was the correspondence which
passed between this devoted couple in the
closing days of their united lives, for
although Mrs. Spurgeon's own letters are
not available, it is clear from a reference
here and there in her husband's replies
that they were of a like loving character.

Christmas was passed by the preacher in
much pain, which, however, did not prevent
him "digging away at books and letters."
Then on New Year's Day, 1891, he writes :
"A happy New Year to you, my sweetest
and best!  I would write it in the biggest
of capitals if that would show how happy I
wish this year to be. . . . I have been for
a drive in the delicious summer sunshine.
Oh, that you had been at my side!  I have
just read your sweet, sweet letter.   You
best-beloved of my heart, how I wish I
could change your weather!  I can only
pray; but prayer moves the hand which
moves winds and clouds.  The Lord Himself comfort you and bear you up under all
troubles, and make up to you, by His own
presence, the absence of health, warmth
and husband!"   Then on Mrs. Spurgeon's

birthday she received a letter in which her husband said: "I trust this will reach you on your own dear birthday. Ten thousand benedictions be upon you! . . . What an immeasurable blessing you have been to me and are still. Your patience in suffering and diligence in service are works of the Holy Spirit in you for which I adore His Name. Your love to me is not only a product of nature, but it has been so sanctified by grace that it has become a spiritual blessing to me. May you still be upheld, and if you may not be kept from suffering, may you be preserved from sinking!"

All this time, although suffering so severely herself, Mrs. Spurgeon was working indefatigably to help others. The Book Fund and the Pastors' Aid Fund were in full swing, and in order to give some relief to the poor of Thornton Heath, who were thrown out of work and in dire straits on account of the prolonged frost, she opened a soup kitchen at "Westwood," and distributed coals freely among the people. C. H. Spurgeon hearing of this, wrote: "I am so glad you feed the poor; spend £10 for me, please; don't stint anything."

At last on February 2nd the patient, apparently much improved in health, started for England, writing to his wife on the same morning a note which concluded with the words, "Blessed be God that we are spared to each other." But the apparent improvement was far from being real or permanent.

This is not the place in which to give a detailed account of C. H. Spurgeon's final days in England. He preached at the Tabernacle for the last time on Sunday morning, June 7th, 1891, and then directly afterwards his illness took an alarming turn, and a fatal issue was feared. Mrs. Spurgeon was an indefatigable nurse, and the sympathy of the whole nation went out to her in her sore trial. Mr. Gladstone wrote: "In my own home, darkened at the present time, I have read with sad interest the daily accounts of Mr. Spurgeon's illness; and I cannot help conveying to you the earnest assurance of my sympathy with you and with him, and of my cordial admiration, not only of his splendid powers, but still more of his devoted and unfailing character. May I humbly commend you and him in all contingencies to the infinite stores of the Divine love and mercy." Many other distinguished people, including a number of the Bishops, also wrote to Mrs. Spurgeon.

The patient did not get better, and on October 26th he started for Mentone, accompanied this time by his wife, as well as by a number of friends. Later, Miss E. H. Thorne, Mrs. Spurgeon's companion and friend, joined the party, and these two ladies took it in turns to nurse the invalid who at first seemed to benefit by the warm Southern sun. But on January 20th serious symptoms set in and Mr. Spurgeon had to take to his bed, from which he never again rose. After remaining unconscious for five days he passed away on January 31st, 1892, in the presence of his wife and four intimate friends. The loss, as may be imagined, was a terrible one for the devoted wife, but she was sustained by the knowledge that sooner or later she would join her husband where there are no more partings. In the death chamber, so soon as the first shock was over, the little party knelt down, and Mr. Harrald, the preacher's private secretary, offered prayer, being followed by Mrs. Spurgeon, who thanked the Lord for the precious treasure so long lent to her, and sought at the throne of grace strength and guidance for the future. Later she was able to cable to her son Thomas, in Australia, "Father in Heaven. Mother resigned." From all parts of the world messages of condolence reached her, those from England including expressions of sympathy from our present King and Queen. The body was removed to this country for burial without delay, and Mrs. Spurgeon sent with the remains a number of palm branches from Mentone to be placed round the coffin while it stood in the Tabernacle.

Mrs. Spurgeon herself remained on the Riviera for some time longer as the guest of Mr. Hanbury, at La Mortola. "There amid the olive-groves and rose-covered terraces," she says, "the dear Master taught me *His* estimate of true affection by recalling to my mind His own words to His disciples, 'If ye loved Me, ye would rejoice, because I go to the Father,' and thus He made me understand that the thought of my darling's everlasting bliss must overcome and banish my own selfish grief and sorrow."

# CHAPTER XIV.

## WIDOWHOOD.

MRS. SPURGEON'S widowhood lasted close upon a dozen years, and in a sense, her life, since 1892, must have been a singularly lonely one, although she had her two sons always near to comfort and cheer her, and the many friends of her late husband were ever ready to meet any wish she might express. Grief, however, did not occupy her to the exclusion of useful and thoughtful work. In fact, her last years were, taking into consideration her growing age and infirmity, her busiest. The Book Fund was never allowed to flag ; the Pastors' Aid Fund was ever ready to help deserving ministers in sore financial straits, and all the other branches of the original organisation were kept in a flourishing condition. Then Mrs. Spurgeon gave a good deal of time to literary work, her *magnum opus* of course being "C. H. Spurgeon's Autobiography, compiled from his Diary, Letters and Records," in which she had the assistance of Mr. Harrald. This, as is generally known, is a monumental work in four large volumes, and it occupied Mrs. Spurgeon

several years in the preparation, all her
husband's correspondence, sermons and
books being carefully sifted in order to
provide the material for the autobiography.
Mrs. Spurgeon herself wrote the chapters
dealing with the home and conjugal life of
her husband, and these in many places
show the pathetic longing she always had
to join him. "Ah! my husband," she says
in one passage, "the blessed earthly ties
which we welcomed so rapturously are dis-
solved now, and death has hidden thee from
my mortal eyes; but not even death can
divide thee from me or sever the love which
united our hearts so closely. I feel it living
and growing still, and I believe it will find
its full and spiritual development only when
we shall meet in the glory-land and worship
together before the throne!" This was
written in 1898, and a comparison with a
passage from her Book Fund report for
1891 will show how time and work had
helped her to a holy resignation in waiting
for the longed-for reunion. "Oh! my
husband, my husband," she wrote in the
earlier year, "every moment of my now
desolate life I wonder how I can live without thee! The heart that for so many
years has been filled and satisfied with thy
love must needs be very empty and stricken
now that thou art gone!"

As a writer, Mrs. Spurgeon had a rare

literary gift, and her style was not unlike that of her husband. It was at C. H. Spurgeon's suggestion that she undertook, while yet Miss Susannah Thompson, to assist him in compiling a little book of extracts from the writings of the Puritan divine, Thomas Brooks. Her lover had asked her to go through "an ancient, rusty-looking book," marking all the paragraphs and sentences that seemed particularly sweet, quaint or instructive, and with much fear and trembling the young girl complied. The result was a small volume entitled "Smooth Stones Taken from Ancient Brooks," and this book, Mrs. Spurgeon's first literary effort, has just been reprinted by Messrs. Passmore and Alabaster.

"Ten Years of My Life in the Service of the Book Fund," and "Ten Years After," have already been referred to, but perhaps the best of Mrs. Spurgeon's literary work will be found in three dainty little devotional volumes entitled, respectively, "A Carillon of Bells to Ring out the Old Truths of ' Free Grace and Dying Love ' " ; "A Cluster of Camphire ; or, Words of Cheer and Comfort for Sick and Sorrowful Souls " ; and "A Basket of Summer Fruit." Each volume is perfect in its way. In a "Carillon of Bells," for instance, one can hear the very bells ringing on every page, and in the whole range of devotional

literature it would be difficult to find anything sweeter or having a truer ring than the
opening words : "' He that spared not His
own Son . . . how shall He not with Him
also freely give us all things.' Dear Lord,
faith's fingers are joyfully touching the
keys of this carillon of sweet bells this morning, and making them ring jubilantly to
the praise of Thy gracious name!

'How shall He not!'
'How shall He not!'
'He that spared not!'
'How shall He not!'

"What a peal of absolute triumph it is!
Not a note of doubt or uncertainty mars the
Heavenly music.    Awake, my heart, and
realize that it is *thy faith* which is making
such    glorious    melody!    Thou    canst
scarcely believe it for gladness?    Yet it is
blessedly true, for the Lord Himself hath
given the grace, and then accepts the
tribute of gratitude and praise which that
grace brings.    Press the tuneful keys again
and again, for faith holds festival to-day and
the joy of assurance is working wonders.

'He that spared not!'
'How shall He not!'

"Hear how the repeated negatives
gloriously *affirm* the fact of His readiness
to bless!    These silver bells have truly the
power to scare away all evil things."

In addition to these volumes, Mrs. Spurgeon is the author of a number of "Westwood Leaflets" on devotional and other topics, and she has been for years past a very frequent contributor to *The Sword and the Trowel,* for the conduct of which until recently she was responsible. Another work in which she took a great and prayerful interest was the selection of the daily texts for "Spurgeon's Illustrated Almanack," and the preparation of that little booklet for publication. For about thirty years she chose the passages of Scripture, and this was no light work, when year after year fresh texts had to be found, which would fulfil the two necessary conditions of being short and also helpful when taken apart from their contexts.

Other kinds of work, too, Mrs. Spurgeon did, and did with all her accustomed zeal. In 1895, for instance, when "Westwood" was being redecorated, she went to Bexhill to stay for a time, and learning that the town possessed no Baptist Chapel, she began to pray and work for the establishment of one. As the result of her efforts a school-chapel was first opened, and in 1897 Mrs. Spurgeon herself laid the foundation-stone of a fine sanctuary, "To the glory of God, and in perpetual remembrance of her beloved husband's blameless life, forty years' public ministry and still continued proclamation of the Gospel by his printed sermons." This chapel was opened free of debt in the following year. In 1899, again, during the collecting of subscriptions for the erection of the present Metropolitan Tabernacle, which was to take the place of the first building, Mrs. Spurgeon not only generously contributed to the Rebuilding Fund, but on a certain day—February 8th —she held a reception in the basement of the Tabernacle, and at one sitting received from those who attended about £6,367 towards the Fund.

In the summer of 1903 Mrs. Spurgeon had a severe attack of pneumonia which prostrated her, and from this she never recovered, being confined to her bed. One or other of her sons visited their mother almost daily to comfort and cheer her in the closing days of her life. Gradually she sank, and in the first week of September the flame of life seemed so feeble that it was expected to flicker out. Even then Mrs. Spurgeon manifested her strong faith in the God whom she had trusted for so long. "Though He slay me, yet will I trust in Him," she said feebly, and quoted the lines :—

> " His love in times past forbids me to think
> He'll leave me at last in trouble to sink."

asking those in the room to complete the verse.

But there was a tenacity of life about this weak woman which was little expected. Week after week she lingered, though getting weaker as each day passed. On October 7th she gave her parting blessing to her son Thomas. "The blessing, the double blessing of your father's God be upon you and upon your brother," she said, and then a few moments later, "Good-bye, Tom; the Lord bless you for ever and ever! Amen." When very near the end she clasped her feeble hands together, and, her face aglow with a heavenly radiance, exclaimed: "Blessed Jesus! Blessed Jesus! I can see the King in His Glory!"

Mrs. Spurgeon passed away peacefully at half-past eight on the morning of Thursday, October 22nd, 1903. She was buried at Norwood Cemetery in the grave where her husband's remains lay, and Pastor Archibald Brown, who spoke such beautiful words at the interment of C. H. Spurgeon, joined with Pastor Sawday in conducting the funeral service over the remains of the great preacher's wife.

# CHAPTER XV.

## CONCLUSION.

MRS. SPURGEON has gone, but her work remains. Her last thoughts were for the Book Fund, and for the poor ministers who are benefited by its aid ; and by her will she left a sum of money for the assistance of the work which owed its inception and its continued success to her untiring zeal. Further, she had expressed a wish that her friend and companion of forty years, Miss E. H. Thorne, should carry on the Book Fund with its various branches, in conjunction with Pastor J. S. Hockey. Miss Thorne has willingly agreed to do this, and her enthusiasm for the work being second only to Mrs. Spurgeon's, it will be a matter for satisfaction to all Christian people who followed with interest the efforts of the deceased lady, that there will be no cessation in the conduct of the Book Fund. C. H. Spurgeon once wrote : "This good work of providing mental food for ministers ought never to cease till their incomes are doubled. May 'Mrs. Spurgeon's Book Fund' become a permanent source of blessing to ministers and churches! " The work must not flag for lack of funds, and as the demand has always been so much greater than the supply, the wherewithal to provide the books cannot be received too quickly. That the devoted woman who originated the Fund, who conducted it with such splendid success for so long, and who gave so generously in her lifetime of her services and substance, has left some money for the Fund, will doubtless only act as an incentive to other "stewards of the Lord" to give liberally, so that this important effort may more and more cope with the need which led to its institution. As a tribute to the memory of Mrs. Spurgeon, what could be better than a gift to the Book Fund which will still bear her name?

If greatness depends upon the amount of good which one does in the world, if it is only another name for unselfish devotion in the service of others—and surely true greatness is all this—then Mrs. C. H. Spurgeon will go down to posterity as one of the greatest women of her time.

# C. H. SPURGEON'S CONVERSION TO CHRIST

Fifteen-year-old Charles Haddon Spurgeon went home for the Christmas holidays at the end of 1849 with a firm determination to visit every place of worship in the town in order to find out the way of salvation. No record exists of exactly how many chapels he attended, but nowhere could he learn what he wanted to know. The ministers expounded the great truths of the Christian faith and their sermons were eminently suited to spiritually-minded people. But what the youth required was knowledge as to how he could get his sins forgiven, and this no man told him.

At last there came a day when the hand of God was unmistakably extended to lead Charles Haddon Spurgeon a way he thought not of. He had intended to go to a certain chapel some distance from his home and set out upon the road. But a heavy snowstorm came on and prevented him from continuing the journey. He turned into an obscure street, and saw at the end of a court a little sanctuary which proved to be the Artillery Street Primitive Methodist Chapel.

This church, hitherto known perhaps to few people even in Colchester, was destined to become world-famed as the result of that visit by the youth of little more than fifteen years. He was not prepossessed in its favour as he entered, for he had always heard that the Primitive Methodists were people who sang so loudly that they made one's head

EXTERIOR OF PRIMITIVE METHODIST CHAPEL, ARTILLERY STREET, COLCHESTER.

INTERIOR OF CHAPEL, SHOWING TABLET OVER PEW WHERE C. H. SPURGEON SAT, JANUARY 6th, 1850.

ache. But even if this were true he cared not so long as they taught him how he might be saved. The remainder of the story shall be told by C. H. Spurgeon himself:

"The minister did not come that morning; he was snowed up, I suppose. At last a very thin-looking man, a shoe-maker, or tailor or something of that sort, went up into the pulpit to preach. Now it is well that preachers should be instructed; but this man was really stupid. He was obliged to stick to his text, for the simple reason that he had little else to say. The text was 'Look unto Me, and be ye saved all the ends of the earth.' He did not even pronounce the words rightly, but that did not matter. There was, I thought, a glimpse of hope for me in that text. The preacher began thus.

'My dear friends, this is a very simple text indeed. It says, "Look." now, lookin' don't take a deal of pains. It ain't liftin' your foot or your finger; it is just "Look." Well, a man needn't go to college to learn to look. You may be the biggest fool and yet you can look. A man needn't be worth a thousand a year to be able to look. Anyone can look; even a child can look. But then the text says, "Look unto Me." Ay!' he said in broad Essex, 'many on ye are lookin' to yourselves, but it's no use lookin' there. You'll never find any comfort in yourselves. Some look to God the Father. No; look to Him by-and-by. Jesus Christ says, "Look unto Me." Some on ye say, "We must wait for the Spirit's workin'." You have no business with that just now. Look to Christ. The text says, "Look unto Me." '

Interior of the Artillery Street Chapel, Colchester, showing tablet over the pew in which C. H. Spurgeon sat on January 6, 1850.

"Then the good man followed up his text in this way: 'Look unto Me; I am sweatin' great drops of blood. Look unto Me; I am hangin' on the cross. Look unto Me; I ascend to Heaven. Look unto Me; I am sittin' at the Father's right hand. O poor sinner, look unto Me! look unto Me!'

"When he had gone to about that length and managed to spin out ten minutes or so he was at the end of his tether. Then he looked at me under the gallery, and I dare say with so few present he knew me to be a stranger. Just fixing his eyes on me, as if he knew all my heart, he said, 'Young man, you look very miserable.' Well, I did; but I had not been accustomed to have remarks made from the pulpit on my personal appearance before. However, it was a good blow, struck right home. He continued, 'And you always will be miserable — miserable in life and miserable in death — if you don't obey my text; but if you obey now, this moment, you will be saved.'

"Then lifting up his hands he shouted, as only a Primitive Methodist could do, 'Young man, look to Jesus Christ. Look! Look! Look! You have nothin' to do but to look and live.' I saw at once the way of salvation. I know not what else he said — I did not take much notice of it — I was so possessed with that one thought. Like as when the brazen serpent was lifted up, the people only looked and were healed, so it was with me. I had been waiting to do fifty things, but when I heard that word 'Look!' what a charming word it seemed to me! Oh! I looked until I could almost have looked my eyes away. There and then the cloud was gone, the darkness rolled away, and that moment I saw the sun; and I could have risen that instant and sung with the most enthusiastic of them of the precious blood of Christ and the simple faith which looks alone to Him.

"That happy day when I found the Saviour and learned to cling to His dear feet was a day never to be forgotten by me. An obscure child, unknown, unheard of, I listened to the Word of God; and that precious text led me to the cross of Christ. I can testify that the joy of that day was utterly indescribable. I could have leaped, I could have danced; there was no expression, however, fanatical, which would have been out of keeping with the joy of my spirit at that hour. Many days of Christian experience have passed since then, but there has never been one which has had the full exhilaration, the sparkling delight which that first day had. I thought I could have sprung from the seat on which I sat, and have called out with the wildest of those Methodist brethren who were present, 'I am forgiven! I am forgiven! A monument of grace! A sinner saved by blood.' I felt that I was an emancipated soul, an heir of Heaven, a forgiven one, accepted in Christ Jesus, plucked out of the miry clay and out of the horrible pit; with my feet upon a rock and my goings established I thought I could dance all the way home. I could understand what John Bunyan meant when he declared he wanted to tell the crows on the ploughed land all about his conversion."

The great event took place on the morning of Sunday, January 6th, 1850.

"LOOK
UNTO ME &
BE YE SAVED
ALL THE ENDS
OF THE
EARTH!"

## CHARLES HADDON SPURGEON
### BORN June 19, 1834
### DIED January 31, 1892

*"He being dead, yet speaketh"* – Hebrews 11:4

C. H. Spurgeon is the most unique minister of the Gospel in English history. For years he has been called "the prince of preachers."

Thousands attended his early ministry in London at the New Park Street Chapel and then later in the new building, Metropolitan Tabernacle, spanning the years from 1854-1892. Millions more who never heard him preach read the weekly sermons as they went forth from the press to the world in many languages. Through these sermons the respect of the Christian world for Spurgeon continues to grow from generation to generation.

Time has justified the prophetic opinion of the late William Robertson Nicoll, who said, *"Our firm belief is that these sermons will continue to be studied with growing interest and wonder; that they will ultimately be accepted as incomparably the greatest contribution to the literature of experimental Christianity that has been made in this century (19th), and that their message will go on transforming and quickening lives after all other sermons of the period are forgotten."*

**D. L. Moody**, the famous evangelist, speaking at a Jubilee Testimonial Service for Spurgeon in 1884, said, *"You are never going to die . . . bear in mind, friends, that our dear brother is to live for ever."*

Moody himself heard and read Spurgeon's sermons before ever becoming a preacher. He said he read everything by Spurgeon he could get his hands on. Moody's Bible Institute and Colportage (now Moody Press) were inspired by Spurgeon's Pastors College and Colportage work. The first and all-time best-selling book by Moody Colportage was *All of Grace* by Spurgeon.

**Child Evangelism Fellowship** also owes its origin to the influence of Spurgeon. In the book, *The Indomitable Mr. O* by Norman Rohrer, the account is related how J. Irvin Overholtzer, when reading a sermon by Spurgeon, was startled by the remark, *"A child of five, if properly instructed, can as readily believe and be regenerated as anyone."* Overholtzer could not get away from the grip of this statement. He decided to make a definite attempt at converting children to Christ and had success. He concluded, *"Child evangelism is real and Spurgeon was right."*

Such stories and testimonies of Spurgeon's influence are unending. At a recent convention of the Christian Booksellers Association, a well-known minister of a large metropolitan area visited the booth of Pilgrim Publications. He said he had traveled several miles just to visit our booth and say "Thanks" to us for reprinting Spurgeon's sermons. He explained that he was a university and seminary graduate, had a Ph.D. degree, had pastored for several years, but only a few months ago he had obtained Spurgeon's sermons and been reading them for the first time. "My preaching has completely changed," he said. "My church has changed, and I feel like I am almost a new man, and have truly just begun to preach."

What is it about Spurgeon's sermons, many of them over one hundred years old, preached to nineteenth century London audiences, that still commands the attention of more readers than the sermons of any other man living or dead? There have been many answers proposed, perhaps all of them valid to a point. But the real answer for each person probably lies in the actual reading and **experiencing** the answer. In some respects, it is like the new birth — "better felt than telt."

Spurgeon was a genius, in addition to the impact of his Christian faith. He was a remarkable "speed reader" and had a "photographic memory." He was also a "natural" orator, a master in the use of scripture, an artist with illustrations, a "wit" with humour and proverbs, carefree and extemporaneous. He lived a godly life, was a man of prayer, and an ardent student of the Bible. But as much as might be said **about** him by admirers, he must be read to be appreciated.

It is doubtful that there is a handful of ministers of evangelical conviction, who have been preaching for a respectable period of time, who have not drawn from the well of inspiration in Spurgeon's sermons.

The late **Dr. Wilbur M. Smith** was known as an authority in the field of Christian literature. Of Spurgeon's sermons, he said, *"If I were given the choice of a set of sermons . . . I would certainly choose those of Charles H. Spurgeon."*

# MISTER MOODY
## ON
# SPURGEON

Remarks Made at a Jubilee Testimonial Service for C. H. Spurgeon in 1884

C. H. SPURGEON : We have need to praise God that he enables the church to carry on all these institutions.    Let us sing hymn No. 7, " Hallelujah for the Cross."

(The hymn was sung.)

I want you now to hear me a moment while I say that the brother who is now about to speak, Mr. Moody, is one whom we all love.    He is not only one whom we all love, but he is evidently one whom God loves.    We feel devoutly grateful to Almighty God for raising him up, and for sending him to England to preach the gospel to such great numbers with such plainness and power.    We shall continue to pray for him when he has gone home.    Among the things we shall pray for will be that he may come back again.    I might quote the language of an old Scotch song with regard to Prince Charlie,—

> " Bonnie Moody's gang awa.
> Will ye no come back again ?
> Better loved ye canna' be,
> Will ye no come back again ? "

Now let us give him as good a cheer as ever we can when he stands up to speak.

Mr. D. L. MOODY : Mr. Spurgeon has said to-night that he has felt like weeping.    I have tried to keep back the tears.    I have not succeeded very well.    I remember, seventeen years ago, coming into this building a perfect stranger.    Twenty-five years ago, after I was converted, I began to read of a young man preaching in London with great power, and a desire seized me to hear him, never expecting that some day I should be a preacher.    Everything I could get hold of in print that he ever said I read.    I knew very little about religious things when I was converted. I did not have what he has had—a praying father.    My father died before I was four years old.    I was thinking of that to-night as I saw Mr. Spurgeon's venerable father here by his side.    He has the advantage of me in that respect, and he perhaps got an earlier start than he would have got if he had not had that praying father.    His mother I have not met, his father I have ; but most good men have praying mothers —God bless them.    In 1867 I made my way across the sea, and if ever there was a sea-sick man for fourteen days, I was that one. The first place to which I came was this building. I was told that I could not get in without a ticket, but I made up my mind to get in somehow, and I succeeded. I well remember seating myself in this gallery. I remember the very seat, and I should like to take it back to America with me. As your dear Pastor walked down to the platform, my eyes just feasted upon him, and my heart's desire for years was at last accomplished. It happened to be the year you preached in the Agricultural Hall. I followed you up there, and you sent me back to America a better man. Then I went to try and preach myself, though at the time I little thought I should ever be able to do so. While I was here I followed Mr. Spurgeon everywhere, and when at home people asked me if I had gone to this and that cathedral, I had to say "No," and confess I was ignorant of them ; but I could tell them something about the meetings addressed by Mr. Spurgeon. In 1872 I thought I would come over again to learn a little more, and again I found my way back to this gallery. I have been here a great many times since, and I never come into the building without getting a blessing to my soul. I think I have had as great a one here to-night as at any other time I have been in this Tabernacle. When I look down on these orphan boys, when I think of the 600 servants of God who have gone out from the College to preach the gospel, of the 1,500 or 2,000 sermons from this pulpit that are in print, and of the multitude of books that have come from the Pastor's pen—(Scripture says of the making of books there is no end, and in his case it is indeed true)—I would fain enlarge upon all these good works, but the clock shows me that if I do, I shall not get to my other meeting in time. But let me just say this, if God can use Mr. Spurgeon why not the rest of us, and why should not we all just lay ourselves at the Master's feet, and say "Send me, use me"? It is not Mr. Spurgeon after all, it is God. He is as weak as any other man away from him. Moses was nothing, but it was Moses' God. Samson was nothing when he lost his strength, but when it came back to him then he was a mighty man ; and so, dear friends, bear in mind that if we can just link our weakness to God's strength we can go forth and be a blessing in the world. Now, there are others to speak, and I have also to hasten away to another meeting, but I want to say to you, Mr. Spurgeon, "God bless you." I know that you love me, but I assure you I love you a thousand times more than you can ever love me, because you have been such a blessing to me, while I have been a very little blessing to you. When I think of a man or woman who has been in this Tabernacle time after time and heard the gospel, I pity them deep down in my heart if they are. found among the lost. I have read your sermons for twenty-five years, and what has cheered my heart has been that in them was no uncertain sound. In closing, let me give you a poem that one of our American Indians wrote. The first line began with "go on," the second line was "go on," and the third line was "go on," and this was all he could write. I say "go on, brother, and God bless you." You are never going to die. John Wesley lives more to-day than when he was in the flesh ; Whitefield lives more to-day than when he was on this earth ; John Knox lives more to-day than at any other period of his life ; and Martin Luther, who has been gone over 400 years, still lives. Bear in mind, friends, that our dear brother is to live for ever. We may never meet together again in the flesh, but by the blessing of God I will meet you up yonder.

# W. ROBERTSON NICOLL'S TRIBUTE TO C. H. SPURGEON

Editor's Note: W. R. Nicoll (1851-1923) was editor of *The British Weekly* and of other notable theological works, including *The Expositor's Greek Testament* and *The Expositor's Bible*. In this article, he says he read through all of Spurgeon's sermons; he later referred to them as a "Body of Divinity."

## [Written Feb. 4, 1892.]

While the great congregations at the Metropolitan Tabernacle assembled on Sunday, their minister was lying unconscious at the doors of dawn. Ere the Sabbath ended he had passed through.. The day for so long of his honourable toil was the day of his sacred rest – the day when he was gathered to the great host of his spiritual children who had gone before.

He has fallen like a tower, and his removal means for many a change in the whole landscape of life. In Scotland he was even more regarded than in England, and in America perhaps his fame stood higher than anywhere else. It is nearly thirty years since he said, not boastfully, but with perfect truth, 'Our word girds the world, and our testimony belts the globe.' His years were not many when he died, but he had lived long, and had maintained to the very last the splendour of his fame.

The popular judgment is often mistaken; but it may be trusted to detect a charlatan *in time*. For the public ear, though easy to gain, is exceedingly hard to keep. It says much both for the power and the essential integrity of Mr. Spurgeon that he caught it when a mere boy, and never lost it for a moment. This was due first of all to his oratorical power.

He was, however, much more than a great orator. The present writer, thrown on one occasion for six months where books were scarce, commenced to read a complete set of the *Metropolitan Tabernacle Pulpit*, and went through all the volumes. We can hardly imagine anyone doing this without receiving a profound and permanent impression. More, the astonishing ability of the preacher is as marked as his eloquence and his sincerity. In this respect he has hardly received justice. Many talk still of his 'crab-apple fertility,' and compare him compassionately with such men as Liddon. In truth, there was no comparison; each excelled in his proper sphere.

It may seem a hard saying, but it cannot be doubted that his theology was a main element in his lasting attraction. Mr. Spurgeon always made salvation a wonderful, a supernatural thing – won through battle and agony and garments rolled in blood. That the blood of God should be one of the ordinary forces of the universe was to him a thing incredible.

This great and hard-won salvation was sure; that is, 'it did not stand in the creature':

Nicoll

## W. Robertson Nicoll's Tribute to Spurgeon

it rested absolutely with God. It was not of man, nor of the will of the flesh. Mr. Spurgeon's hearers had many of them missed all the prizes of life; but God did not choose them for the reasons that move man's preference; else their case were hopeless. Their election was of grace.

And as He chose them, He would keep them. The perseverance of the saints is a doctrine without meaning to the majority of Christians. But many a poor girl with the love of Christ and goodness in her heart, working her fingers to the bone for a pittance that just keeps her alive, with the temptations of the streets around her, and the river beside her, listened with all her soul when she heard that Christ's sheep could never perish. Many a struggling tradesman tempted to dishonesty; many a widow with penury and loneliness before her, were lifted above all, taught to look through and over the years coming thick with sorrow and conflict, and anticipate a place in the Church Triumphant.

Personally Mr. Spurgeon was keenly alive to the humorous side of things — witty, brilliant, and sometimes exuberant. But as is so often the case with such natures, his thought turned habitually to the wistful, pathetic, melancholy side of life.

In manner he was scrupulously and even anxiously courteous. But we must leave many things unsaid. Never has a man with such an experience appeared in the Christian Church — never one who has addressed so many of his fellow creatures on the things of God — never one the obvious results of whose ministry have been so great. 'I shall never hear you calling,' we say as we think of that unforgotten voice. But its echoes will linger when the strife of tongues is passing.

The continued life and power of his printed sermons show that his oratory, noble as it was, was not the first thing. Our firm belief is that these sermons will continue to be studied with growing interest and wonder; that they will ultimately be accepted as incomparably the greatest contribution to the literature of experimental Christianity that has been made in this century, and that their message will go on transforming and quickening lives after all other sermons of the period are forgotten.

## THE NEW PARK STREET PULPIT (1855-1860) and
## THE METROPOLITAN TABERNACLE PULPIT (1861-1917)

In 1854, when still a teen-ager, C. H. Spurgeon left his flourishing pastorate at the country village of Waterbeach to pastor London's New Park Street Chapel. Among his predecessors had been Benjamin Keach, John Gill and John Rippon, "giants" of the faith. When Spurgeon was first invited to the church, he felt there had been a mistake, and so did not immediately respond; however, there had been no mistake, as history has demonstrated.

NEW PARK-STREET CHAPEL
The first building in which Mr. Spurgeon preached in London.

Among the members of the church was Mr. Joseph Passmore, who was a printer. Recognizing the amazing gifts of the young nineteen-year-old lad and the immense opportunity for the spread of the sermons by the printed page, Passmore suggested the publication of a weekly *"penny pulpit,"* a common method of sermon distribution in the 19th century.

"With much fear and trembling," Spurgeon says, he gave consent. The first sermon published was preached on January 7, 1855, under the title, *The New Park Street Pulpit.* The weekly "penny pulpit" met with immediate success. At the end of the year, the weekly sermons were then published collectively as one volume. This method continued through 1860 and into 1861 when Spurgeon led the church into the newly constructed Metropolitan Tabernacle. The "penny pulpit" then was called *The Metropolitan Tabernacle Pulpit.* Week-by-week and year-by-year the "penny pulpits" and yearly volumes went forth, their number now innumerable because no accurate publishing records were kept, neither of the early years nor of the many ways by which they were circulated. Many newspapers even carried the sermons and they were also translated in other nations.

Spurgeon died in 1892, but the sermon publication continued, using the stenographically-recorded messages delivered at evening services and during the week. They finally ceased in 1917 due to the hardship of wartime conditions.

The complete set of volumes was sixty-three, counting the months into 1917 in which they were published.

The total number of sermons in the 63 volumes is 3,561.

These are all-time records! Sixty-two and one-third consecutive years, 3,241 consecutive weeks, 3,561 consecutive sermons! Will such a record ever be matched?

Both B. H. Carroll and W. R. Nicoll proclaimed the set to be *"a complete body of systematic theology,"* a veritable *"Body of Divinity."*

It is with great joy and thanksgiving to God that in His providence the present publishers have been enabled to find and republish the complete series of Spurgeon's sermons. It is our prayer that the sermons will live long after we have left the scene of life, to bless succeeding generations as they have in the past and present.

— Bob L. Ross, Director —

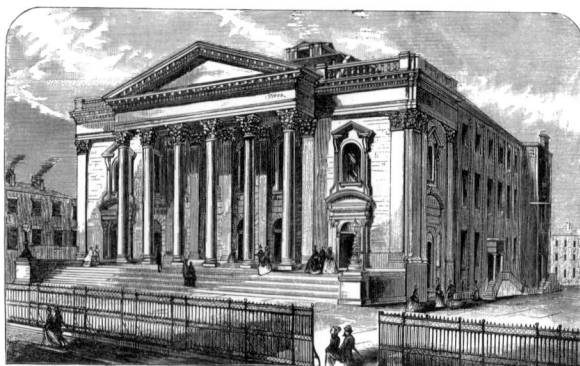

# C. H. SPURGEON'S
# 𝔐etropolitan 𝔗abernacle 𝔓ulpit

## By DR. WILBUR M. SMITH

*NOTE: This article was prepared by Dr. Smith in July, 1969, for publication in his MOODY MONTHLY column, "In the Study." Note particularly Dr. Smith's estimation of Spurgeon's sermons as expressed in the second paragraph of the article.*

One of the most remarkable undertakings of reprinting rich Christian literature, long out of print, has just been announced by Pilgrim Publications of Pasadena, Texas. They have just issued the first volume (1861) of the 63 volume set of the *New Park Street and Metropolitan Tabernacle Pulpit.*

**I would say, without any hesitation at all, that these volumes form the greatest collection of sermons by one minister of the Word of God that we have in the English language.**

It is really quite amazing when one thinks of it that no one today is reprinting the truly great sermons of H. P. Liddon, Bishop Westcott, Hugh Macmillan, R. W. Church, etc. But Spurgeon's sermons have been reprinted over and over again. Dr. John Brown was exactly right when in his Lyman Beecher's lecture at Yale in 1899, he referred to Mr. Spurgeon's ministry as "a success certainly unparalleled in England since the days of Whitefield and Wesley."

When Charles H. Spurgeon came to London, in 1855, to begin his amazing metropolitan ministry, he could have had no premonition whatsoever that in the years that were before him, he would be having as fellow-laborers the greatest galaxy of preachers Britain has ever known for a given period of forty years. **H. P. Liddon** (1829-1890) would be delivering his profound sermons to great audiences at St. Paul's Cathedral; **Joseph Parker** (1830-1902) would be expounding the Scriptures at City Temple; **F. W. Farrar** (1831-1903), with not such a biblical emphasis, would often be heard at Westminster Abbey; and **Hugh Price Hughes** (1847-1902), of whose ministry at West London

**C. H. SPURGEON'S First Words at the Tabernacle**

I WOULD PROPOSE THAT THE SUBJECT OF THE MINISTRY IN THIS HOUSE, AS LONG AS THIS PLATFORM SHALL STAND, & AS LONG AS THIS HOUSE SHALL BE FREQUENTED BY WORSHIPPERS, SHALL BE THE PERSON OF **JESUS CHRIST.** I AM NEVER ASHAMED TO AVOW MYSELF A CALVINIST; I DO NOT HESITATE TO TAKE THE NAME OF BAPTIST; BUT IF I AM ASKED WHAT IS MY CREED, I REPLY, "IT IS JESUS CHRIST." MY VENERATED PREDECESSOR, DR. GILL, HAS LEFT A BODY OF DIVINITY, ADMIRABLE & EXCELLENT IN ITS WAY; BUT THE BODY OF DIVINITY TO WHICH I WOULD PIN & BIND MYSELF FOR EVER, GOD HELPING ME, IS NOT HIS SYSTEM, OR ANY OTHER HUMAN TREATISE; BUT CHRIST JESUS, WHO IS THE SUM & SUBSTANCE OF THE GOSPEL, WHO IS IN HIMSELF ALL THEOLOGY, THE INCARNATION OF EVERY PRECIOUS TRUTH, THE ALL-GLORIOUS PERSONAL EMBODIMENT OF THE WAY, THE TRUTH, & THE LIFE.

Mission it is said "took London by storm." **F. B. Meyer** began his influential work at Regents Park Chapel in 1888. By leaving London one could go to Manchester and hear **Alexander Maclaren** (1826-1910); to Birmingham and hear **R. W. Dale** (1829-1895), or on to Edinburgh and hear **Alexander Whyte** (1836-1921). (It is interesting to note that seven of these remarkably gifted preachers were born within a period of eight years, 1829-1836). All of those men drew great crowds (though not all of them held large audiences to the end), but none as great as Mr. Spurgeon.

**C. H. SPURGEON'S Last Words at the Tabernacle**

If you wear the livery of Christ, you will find Him so meek and lowly of heart that you will find rest unto your souls. He is the most magnanimous of captains. There never was His like among the choicest of princes He is always to be found in the thickest part of the battle. When the wind blows cold He always takes the bleak side of the hill, The heaviest end of the cross lies ever on His shoulders. If He bids us carry a burden, He carries it also. If there is anything that is gracious, generous, kind, and tender, yea lavish and superabundant in love, you always find it in Him. His service is life, peace, Joy. Oh, that you would enter on it at once! God help you to enlist under the banner of **JESUS CHRIST!**

C. H. SPURGEON'S LAST WORDS AT THE TABERNACLE, JUNE 7, 1891.

# C. H. Spurgeon's Sermon Set:
## COMMENDATIONS and REVIEWS

BIBLIOTHECA SACRA (Dallas Seminary): "These sermons reveal even in cold type the charm, eloquence, and spiritual power of this giant of the pulpit. Although delivered long ago, the sermons have the same relevance, pungency, and convicting power as when first delivered to the large audiences which heard him in the Metropolitan Tabernacle in London. Undoubtedly this will be, as claimed by the publishers, one of the greatest sets of sermons in the history of the church."

BAPTIST QUARTERLY (England): "Pilgrim Publications has recently undertaken the mammoth task of republishing the 57 volumes of Spurgeon's sermons, as well as other titles of his. Of Spurgeon, the preacher, we say 'Take and read.' The best way to discover the real Spurgeon is to read his sermons. The range of his preaching is remarkable. Spurgeon lived his own words."

REVIEW AND EXPOSITOR (Louisville Seminary): "Pilgrim Publications is making Spurgeon's works available to those who are being caught up in a renewed interest in this master preacher. Though in many ways Charles Spurgeon was a child of his own times, his sermons possess a surprising timelessness. His warm devotion to Jesus Christ, his common sense, his homely wit, and his informal style combine to make his sermons a delight to read today."

BOOKSTORE JOURNAL (Christian Booksellers Association): "Just to know the stature and reputation of the author is sufficient without any man's recommendation! Thousands give testimony to the value of Spurgeon's sermons in their ministry and upon individual lives. His dual ministry, that of the spoken and written word, is timeless, speaking of the perennial power of the Word of God as it speaks to man at all times."

MOODY MONTHLY (Moody Bible Institute): "One of the most remarkable undertakings of reprinting rich Christian literature, long out of print, has been announced by Pilgrim Publications of Pasadena, Texas . . . I would say, without any hesitation at all, that these 57 volumes (Metropolitan Tabernacle Pulpit) form the greatest collection of sermons by one minister of the Word of God that we have in the English language" (Dr. Wilbur M. Smith).

CHRISTIANITY TODAY: "For those who were not privileged to be numbered among his (Spurgeon's) congregation at New Park Street Chapel or later at the Metropolitan Tabernacle, it is indeed fortunate that the sermons of this master of the pulpit were recorded on the printed page. Spurgeon's sermons are filled with the necessary ingredients of good preaching and have set a standard rarely reached in today's pulpits . . . It is indeed gratifying that this incomparable series of sermons is being made available once again."

SWORD OF THE LORD (John R. Rice): "We are glad that Pilgrim Publications, in Pasadena, Texas, is now reprinting Spurgeon's sermons. Previously, a selection of twenty volumes of Spurgeon's sermons was published widely; they are now out of print. However, these were only selected sermons from the whole. We are glad that all of Spurgeon's sermons will now be reproduced just as originally published by Spurgeon in Spurgeon's day."

AUSTRALIAN BAPTIST: "Above all else we commend Spurgeon because of the Biblical content of his sermons. Here is sound doctrine, the doctrines of grace. Here is white-hot evangelism, and at the same time evidence of the heart of a loving pastor. Preachers and evangelists will find inspiration for their ministry in these volumes."

NEW LIFE (Australia): "The republication of these volumes could prove to be a powerful preservative for evangelical Christianity. These volumes complete and unabridged contain some of the finest preaching this world has ever heard. How much one would like to say! The best thing is that you procure a copy and delve into its heart-warming and inspiring contents."

EVANGELICAL BAPTIST (Canada): "Charles H. Spurgeon, by general agreement, was one of the great preachers of the ages. His weekly sermons were avidly read as they came from the publisher. Then, each year, the annual volume appeared under the title, 'Metropolitan Tabernacle Pulpit.' Those volumes are to be printed now just as they appeared from the presses in former time."

PRAIRIE OVERCOMER (Prairie Bible Institute): "Pilgrim Publications has launched what must be one of the most ambitious reprint projects of the twentieth century. We refer to the republication of C. H. Spurgeon's Metropolitan Tabernacle Pulpit sermons in their original form, completely unabridged."

# OUTSTANDING BOOKS
## BY C. H. SPURGEON

*

These great books and many more by the late C. H. Spurgeon have been reprinted from the original editions by Pilgrim Publications. P.O. Box 66, Pasadena, Texas 77501.

# 𝕮. 𝕳. Spurgeon's
# 𝔄utobiography

## COMPILED FROM

## HIS DIARY, LETTERS, AND RECORDS

The FOUR Original, Unedited Volumes
Published by Passmore & Alabaster
**FIRST TIME** to ever be reprinted.

•

Hundreds of Photographs

•

**FOUR** Volumes in **TWO** Large Books

•

BLACK Bindings, GOLD-STAMPED
on Spine and Front Cover

•

Volumes 1 & 2, 768 pages
Volumes 3 & 4, 784 pages

•

Large 6″ x 9″ Format

These great books and many more by the late C. H. Spurgeon have been reprinted from the original editions by Pilgrim Publications. P.O. Box 66, Pasadena, Texas 77501.

# SETS BY CHARLES HADDON SPURGEON (1834-1892)

Pilgrim Publications is the only source for exact reprints of sets by C. H. Spurgeon which were originally published by Spurgeon's London publisher, Passmore & Alabaster, in the last century. All books are unedited and unabridged.

● THE NEW PARK STREET PULPIT consists of the first six volumes of the Spurgeon sermon series, covering the years 1855-1860, sermons #1-347. Our edition is in three large double-volumes, two years to each book.

● THE METROPOLITAN TABERNACLE PULPIT consists of volume 7 thru volume 63 of the Spurgeon sermon series, covering years 1861 thru 1917, sermons #348-3561.

● THE TREASURY OF DAVID is the seven-volume commentary on the Book of Psalms, twenty years in the making and the most extensive work ever accomplished on the Psalms.

● THE SWORD AND THE TROWEL is a series of volumes containing the miscellaneous writings of Spurgeon as published in his monthly magazine, beginning in 1865. Sermons, tracts, editorials, book reviews, conference addresses, outlines, letters, and other materials are reprinted unedited.

● LECTURES TO MY STUDENTS consists of the original four volumes in this series and for the first time reprinted unabridged in one durable clothbound edition.

● C. H. SPURGEON'S AUTOBIOGRAPHY consists of the original four large volumes published under the auspices of Mrs. Spurgeon and his secretary, J. W. Harrald. Reprinted directly from the P & A original set; includes all the hundreds of photographs. Our edition combines the four volumes in two large clothbound, gold-stamped 6" x 9" books. First time ever to be reprinted.

Ask for these books at your local Christian book store. Consult a current price list (free on request) for current prices.

Pilgrim Publications, P. O. Box 66, Pasadena, Texas 77501
Phone (713)477-2329 - Fax (713)477-7561

## RARE REPRINTS
## By LARRY HARRISON, BOOKSELLER

Abe Lincoln's Assassination – Harris, McCarty ............ $ 6.00
American Revivals – Thompson ............ $ 3.00
Anecdotes and Illustrations – D. L. Moody ............ $ 7.00
Autobiography of Peter Cartwright ............ $ 7.00
B. R. Lakin  (Biography) ............ $ 3.00
Baptist History in the South ............ $ 5.00
Baptist Story, The – Davis ............ $ 6.00
Bible Makes Us Baptists, The – Bamford ............ $ 7.00
Billy Bray, the King's Son – Bourne ............ $ 3.00
Brother Sheffey – Barbery ............ $ 5.00
C. H. Spurgeon's Sermons Notes – Fuller ............ $ 7.00
C. I. Scofield – Biography by Trumbull ............ $ 6.00
Chaplains in Gray – Pitts ............ $ 5.00
Charles Alexander  (Biography) ............ $ 6.00
Charles Spurgeon ............ $ 3.00
Christie's Old Organ – Walton ............ $ 3.00
David Brainerd – His Message for Today – Smith ............ $ 3.00
Death of a Book Seller – Farmer ............ $ 3.00
Dying Testimonies of Saved and Unsaved – Shaw ............ $ 6.00
Great Love Stories of the Bible – Billy Sunday ............ $ 5.00
Great Outlines ............ $ 3.00
Great Sermons – Jonathan Edwards, D. L. Moody, etc. ............ $ 3.00
Great Sermons from Yesteryear – Moody, Spurgeon, etc. ............ $ 5.00
Hosea – Commentary by G. Campbell Morgan ............ $ 5.00
How on Earth Can I be Spiritual – Wemp ............ $ 5.00
How to Work for Christ – R. A. Torrey ............ $ 8.00
Hyman Appelman Outlines ............ $ 3.00
J. Frank Norris I Have Known – L. Entzminger ............ $ 5.00

John G. Paton – Hero of the South Seas ............ $ 3.00
John Jasper – Hatcher (Biography) ............ $ 5.00
John Ploughman's Talk – Spurgeon ............ $ 4.00
John Wesley's Awakening ............ $ 3.00
Last of the Giants – Harry Rimmer ............ $ 5.00
Life & Sayings of Sam Jones – Mrs. Jones ............ $ 7.00
Marion and His Men – DeMorgan ............ $ 5.00
Martyrs of the Catacombs ............ $ 3.00
Moody's Latest Sermons ............ $ 3.00
Practical Pastoring – Wemp ............ $ 6.00
Preacher and His Preaching – Riley ............ $ 3.00
Private Devotional Lives of Finney, Moody, Spurgeon ............ $ 4.00
Quotes and Quaint Stories – Chamberlain ............ $ 3.00
Ray's Baptist Succession – D. B. Ray ............ $ 7.00
Real Billy Sunday, The – Brown (Biography) ............ $ 6.00
Religion in Lee's Army – Rev. Jones ............ $ 3.00
Robert Hardy's Seven Days – C. Sheldon ............ $ 3.00
Sam Jones' Sermons ............ $ 3.00
Scarlet Thread Through the Bible – Criswell ............ $ 3.00
Sergeant York – Last of the Longhuners – Skeyhill ............ $ 6.00
Sermons of George Whitefield ............ $ 3.00
So Great the Burden – Ruth Harrison ............ $ 3.00
Soul Winning Sermons – G. B. Vick ............ $ 3.00
Stars of the Twilight – Scott ............ $ 5.00
Stories of Civil War Songs – Emurien ............ $ 3.00
Twenty Years with Billy Sunday – Rodeheaver ............ $ 5.00
Uncle Bud Robinson – Chapman ............ $ 5.00
We Thought We Heard the Angels Sing – Whitaker ............ $ 4.00
Words to Winners of Souls – Horatius Bonar ............ $ 3.00

Send Check or Money Order to: Larry Harrison,
P. O. Box 8, St. John IN 46373.  Add 10% for Postage – (219) 644-8869